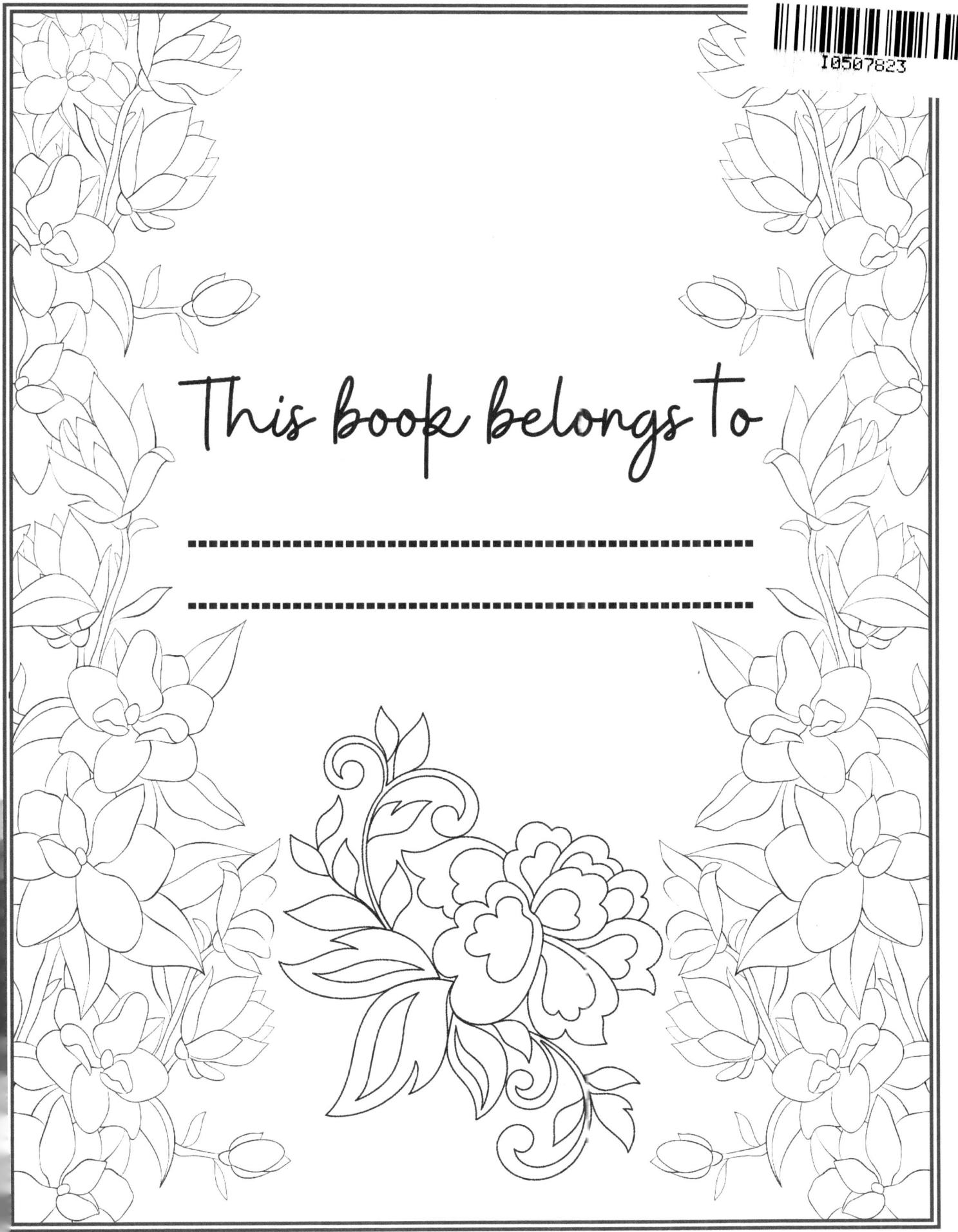

Copyright © 2020 by Blueberry Publishing House

Cover Design by Blueberry Publishing House

All rights reserved. No part of this book may be reproduced without written permission of the copyright owner, except for the use of limited quotations for the purpose of book reviews.

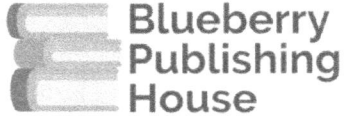

Follow us

amazon.com/author/blueberry

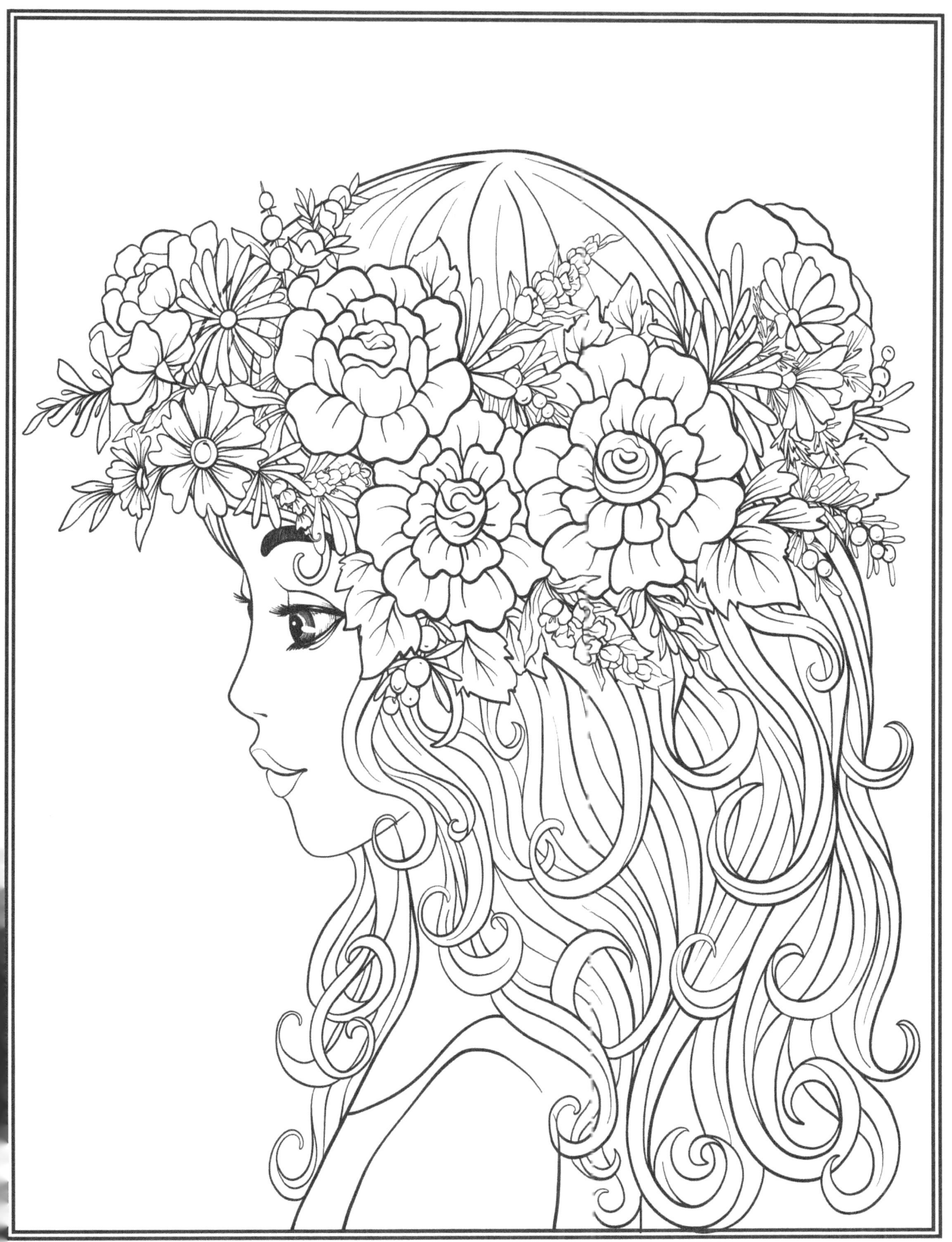

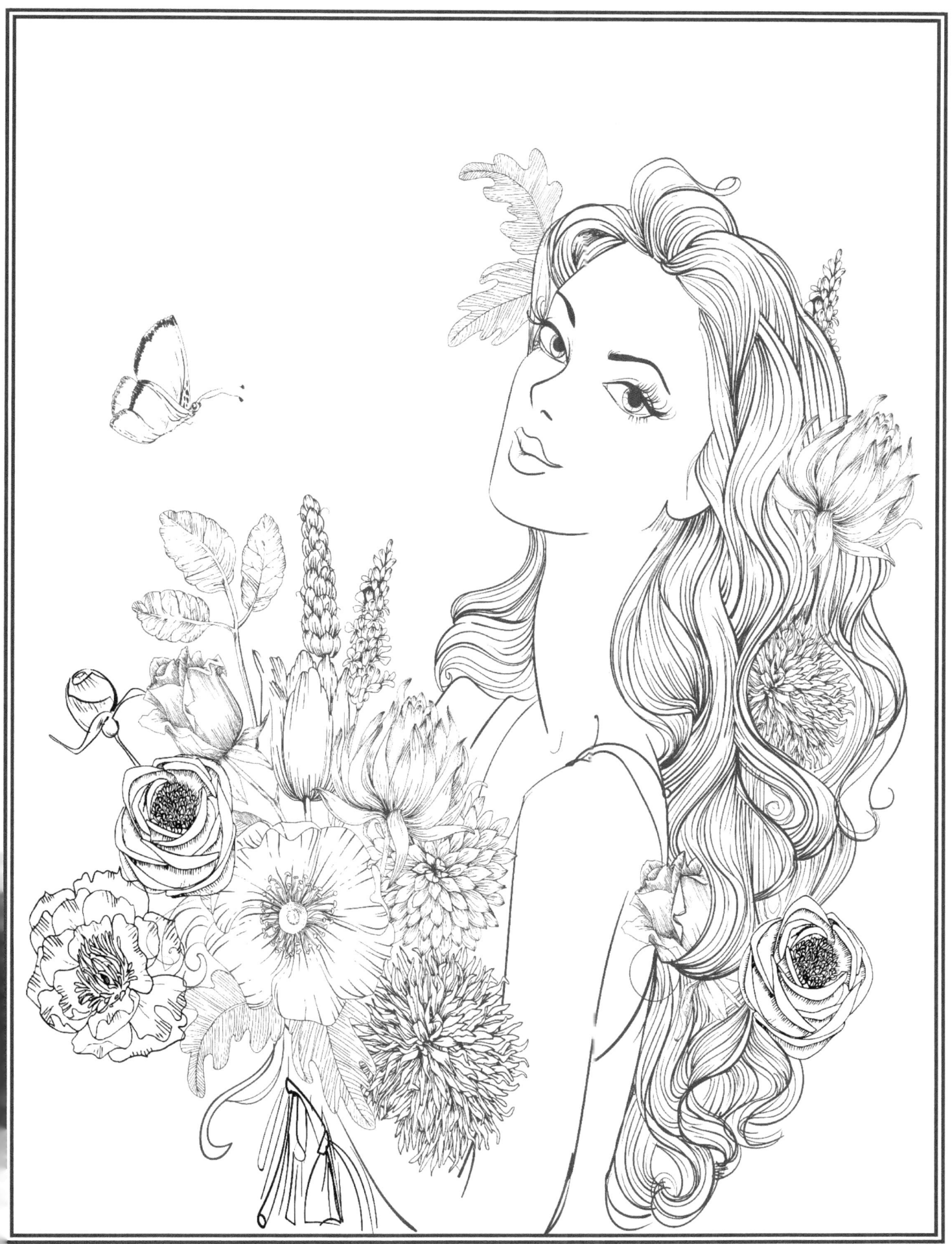

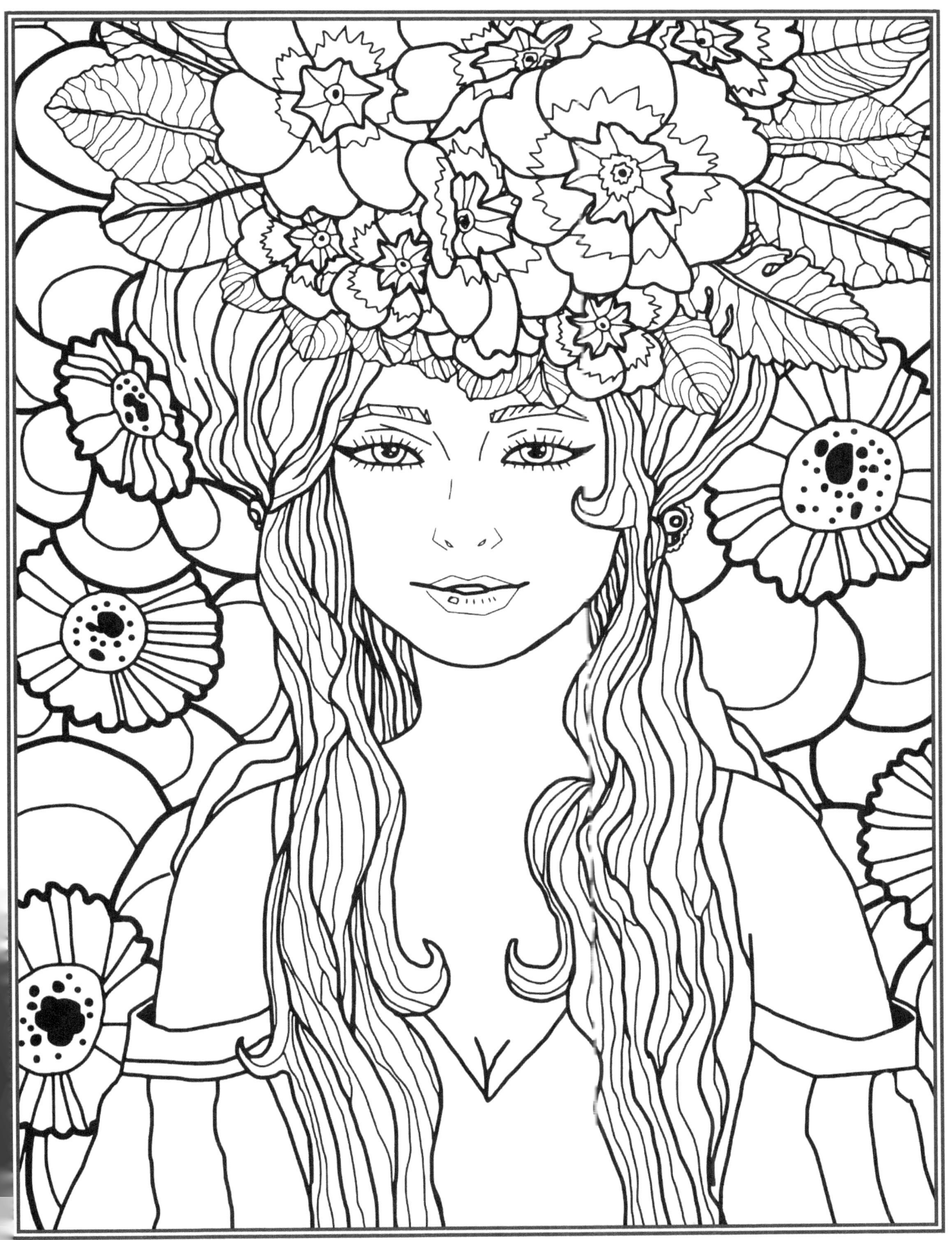

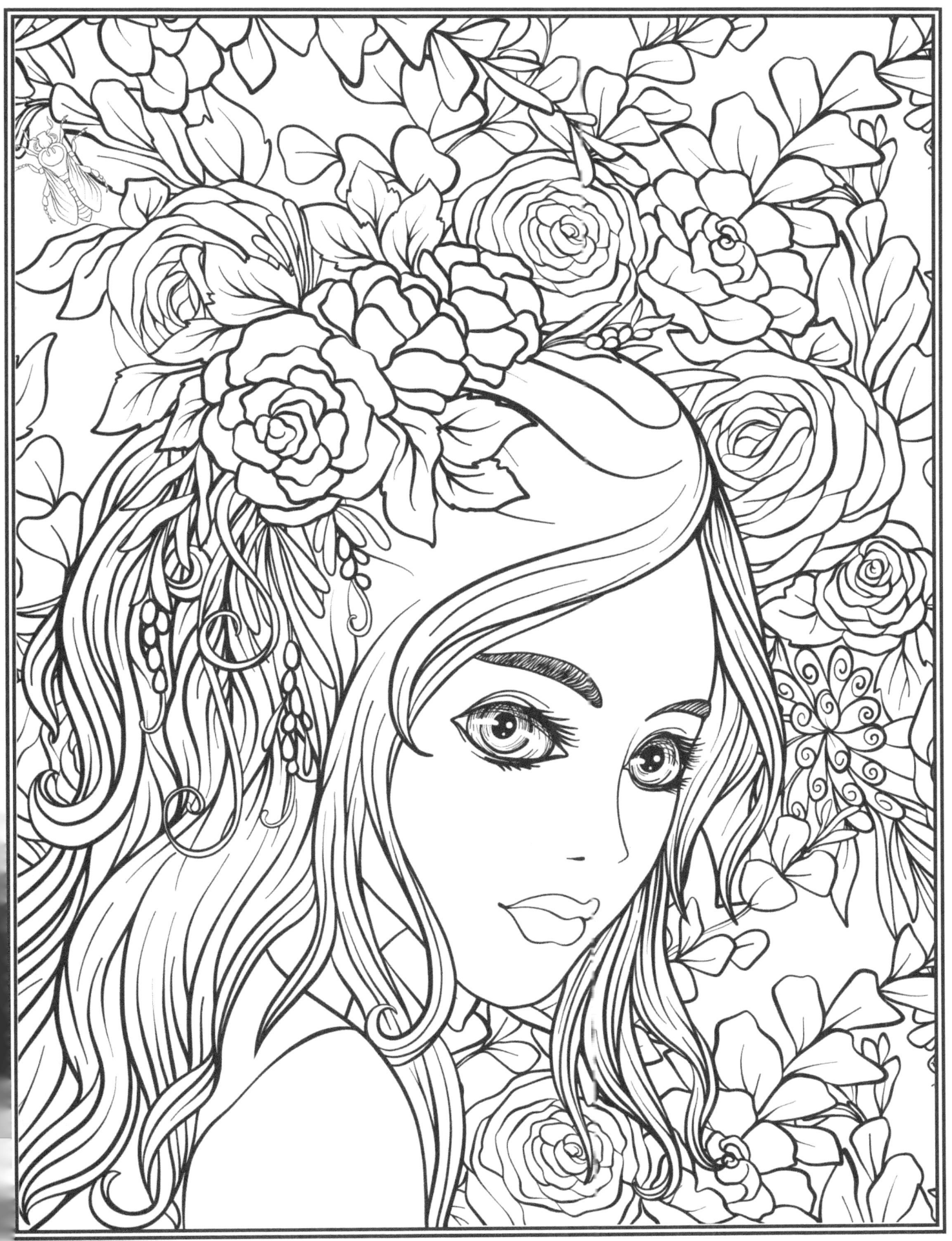

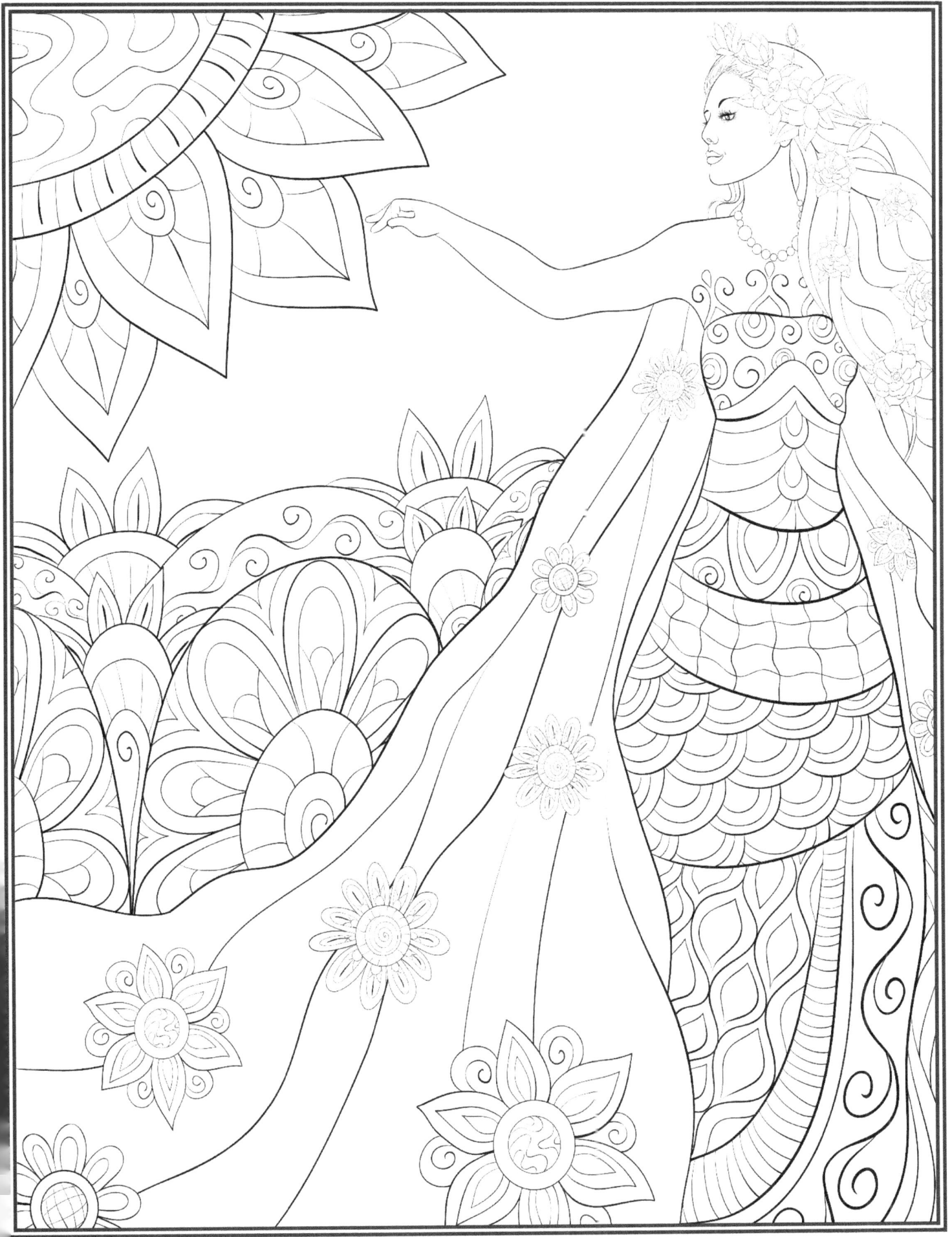

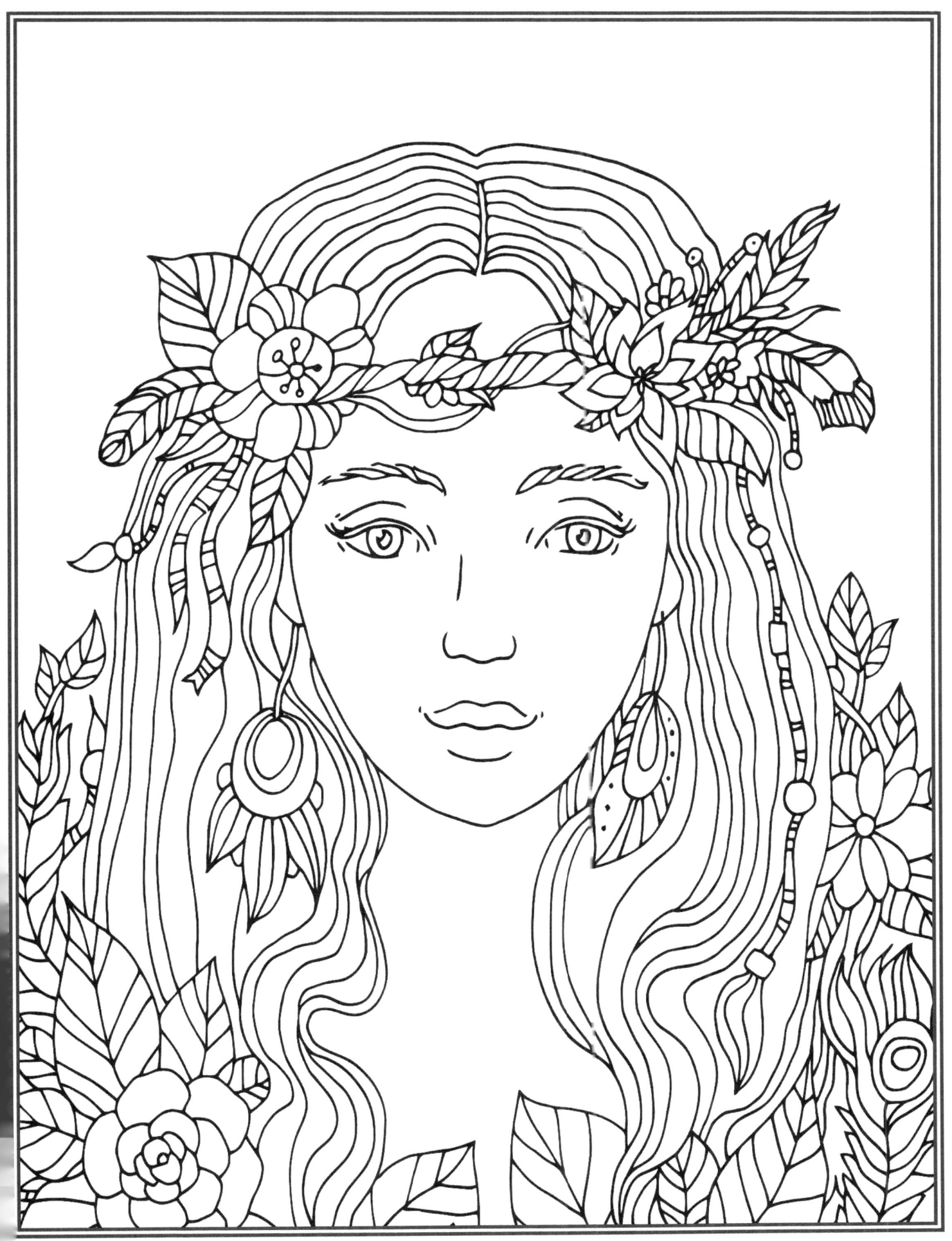

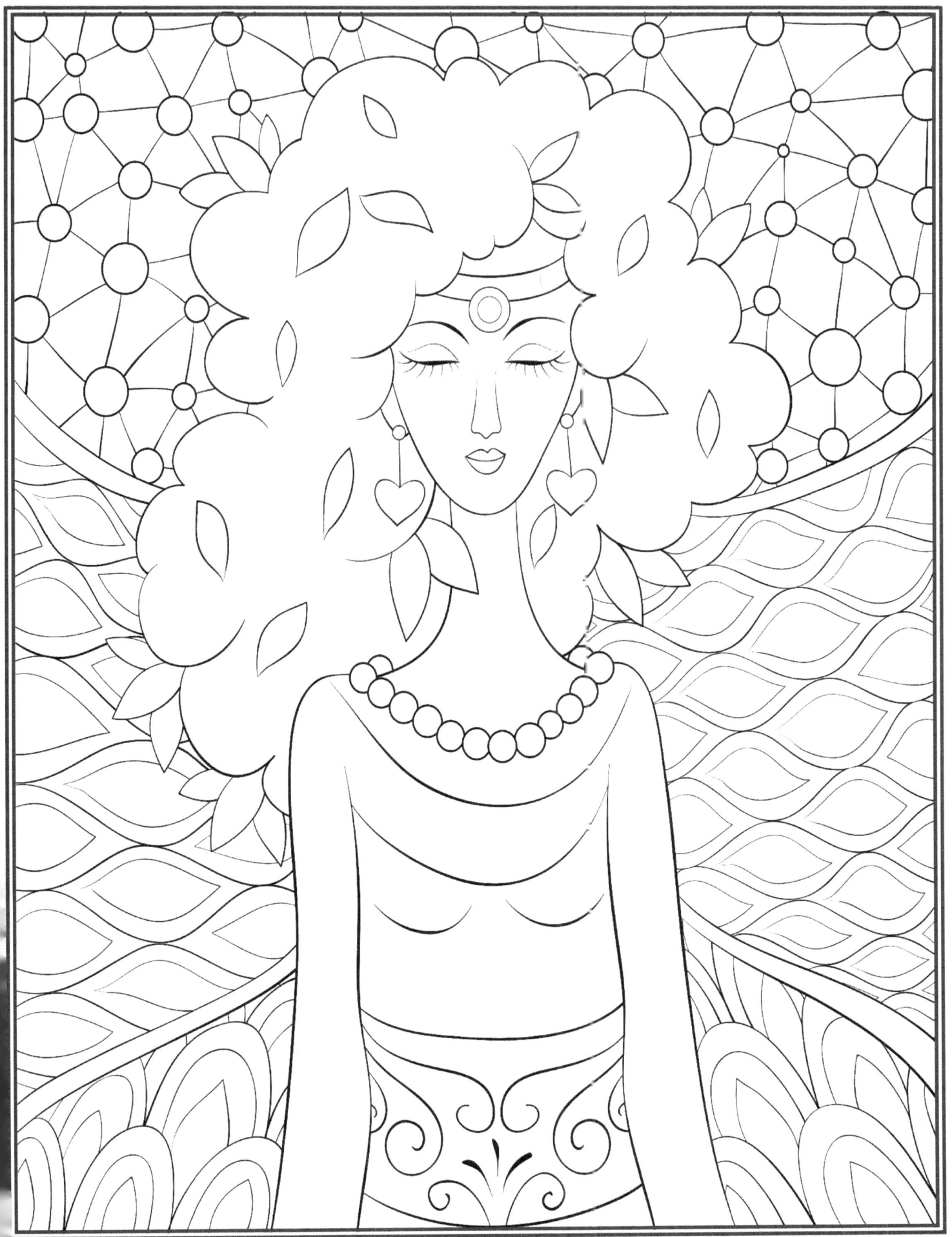

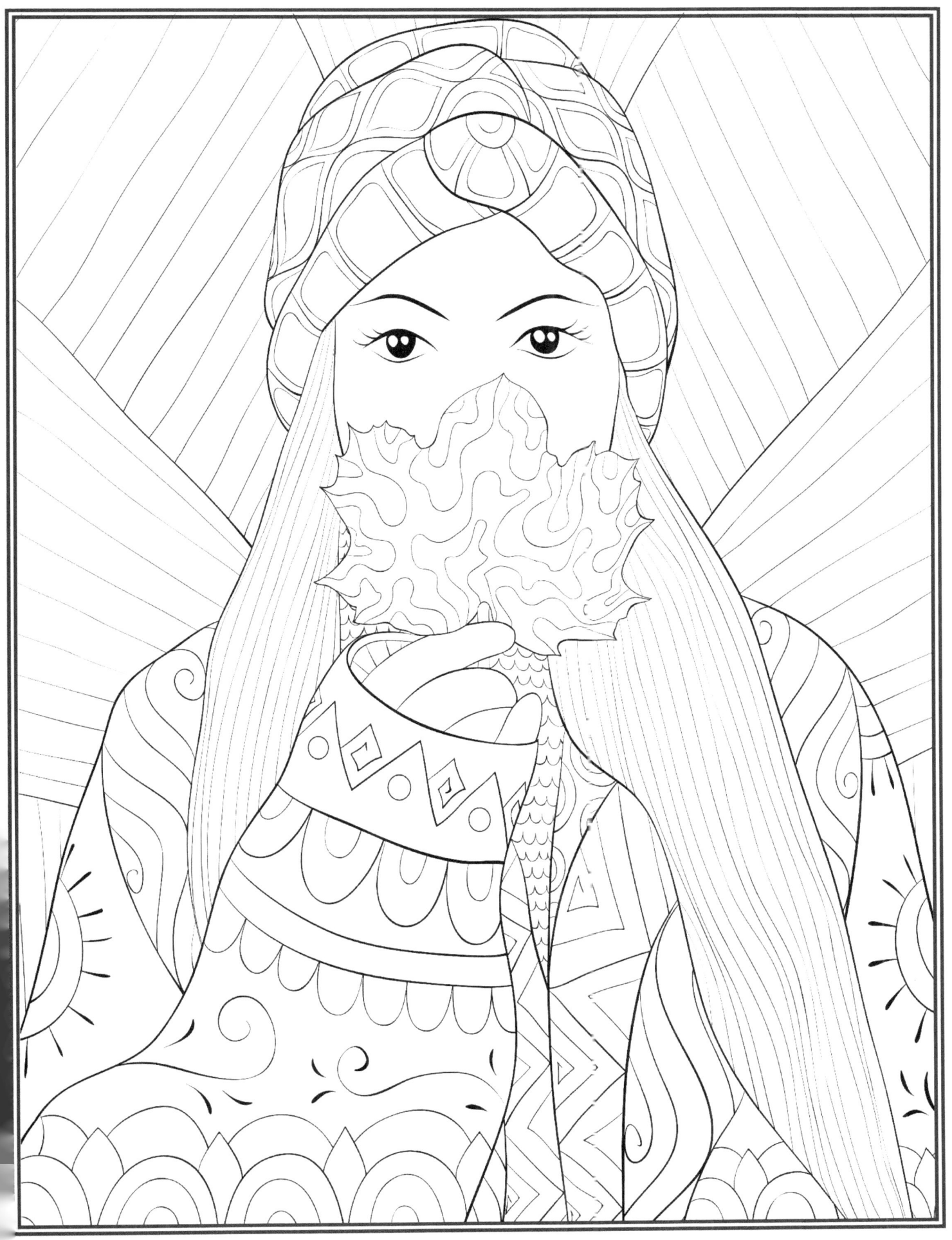

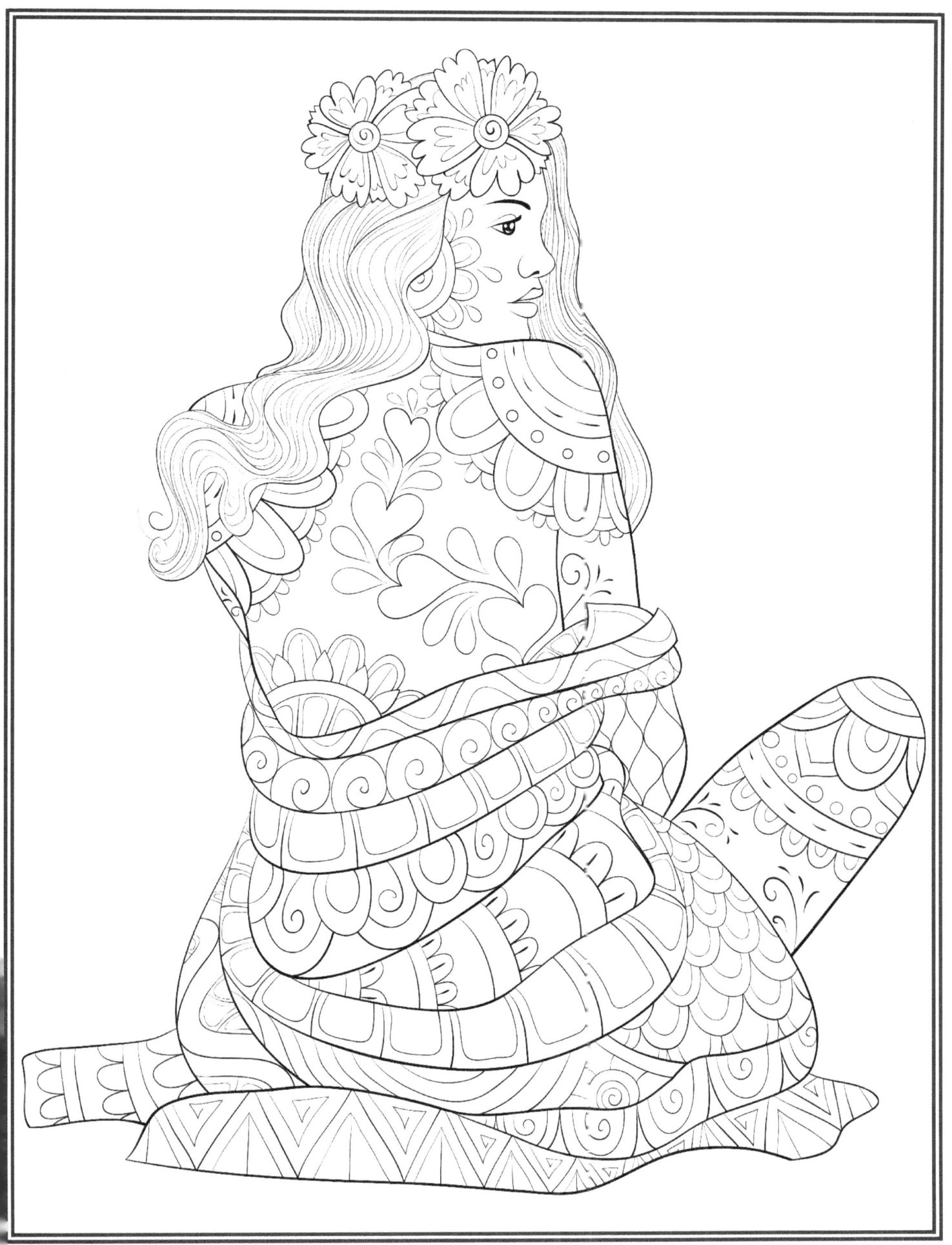

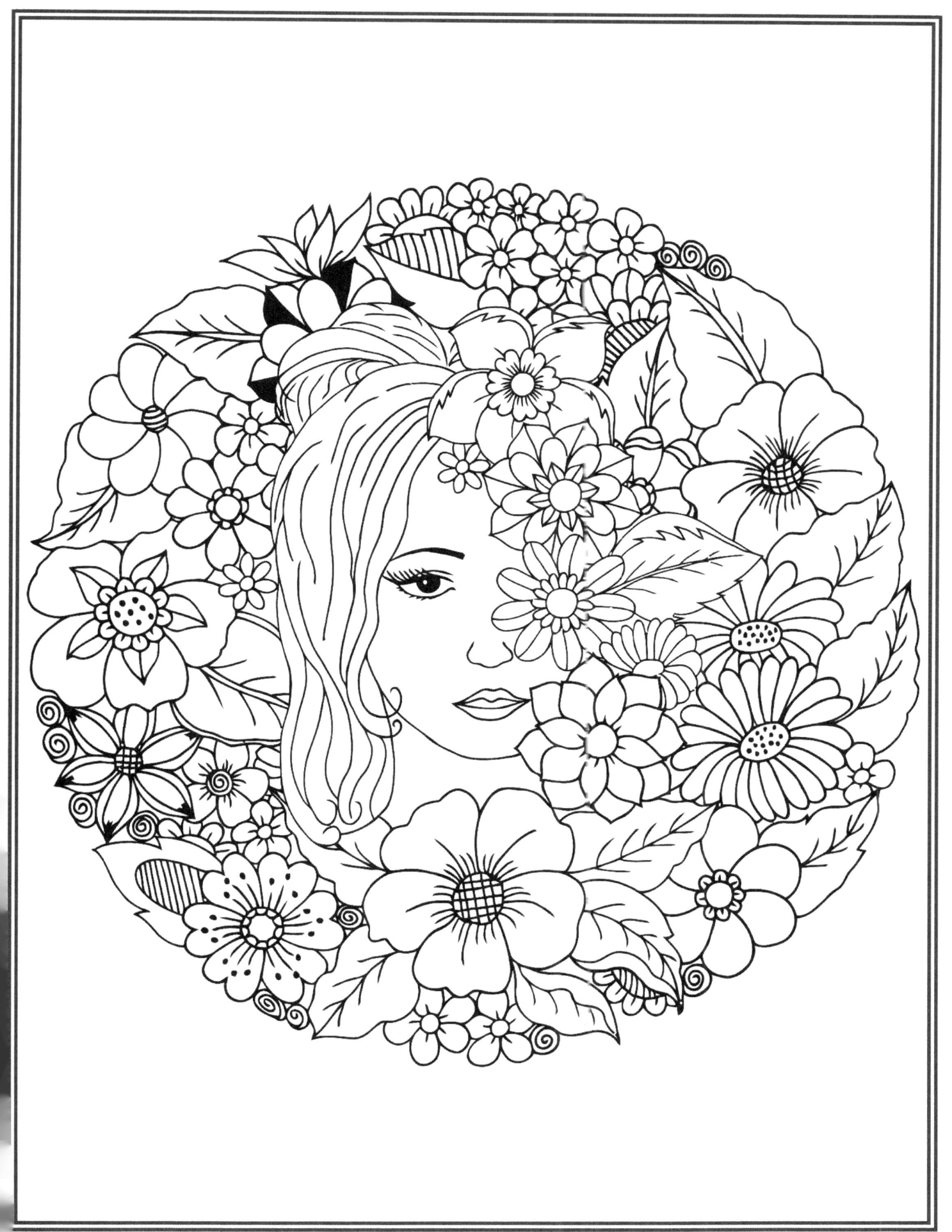

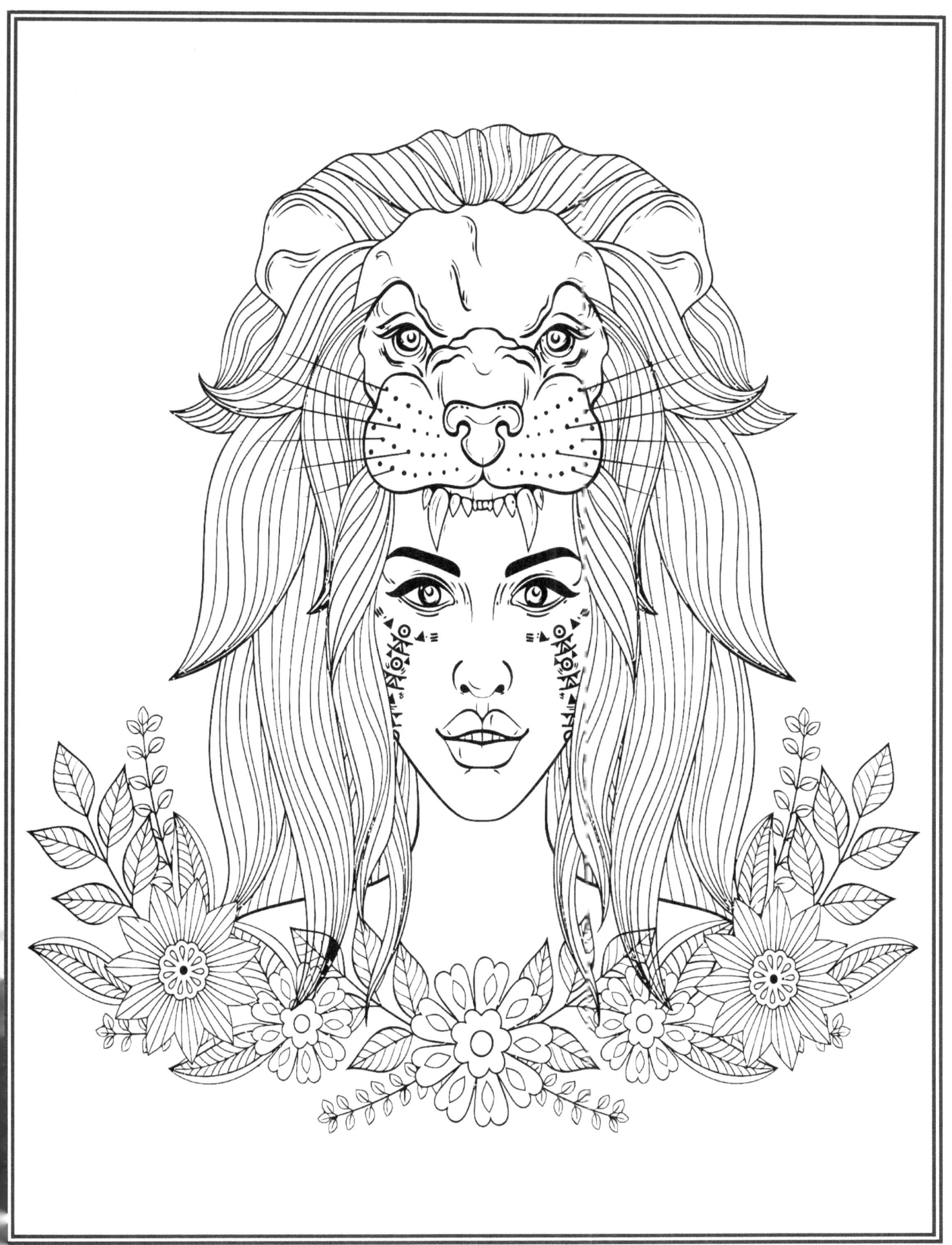

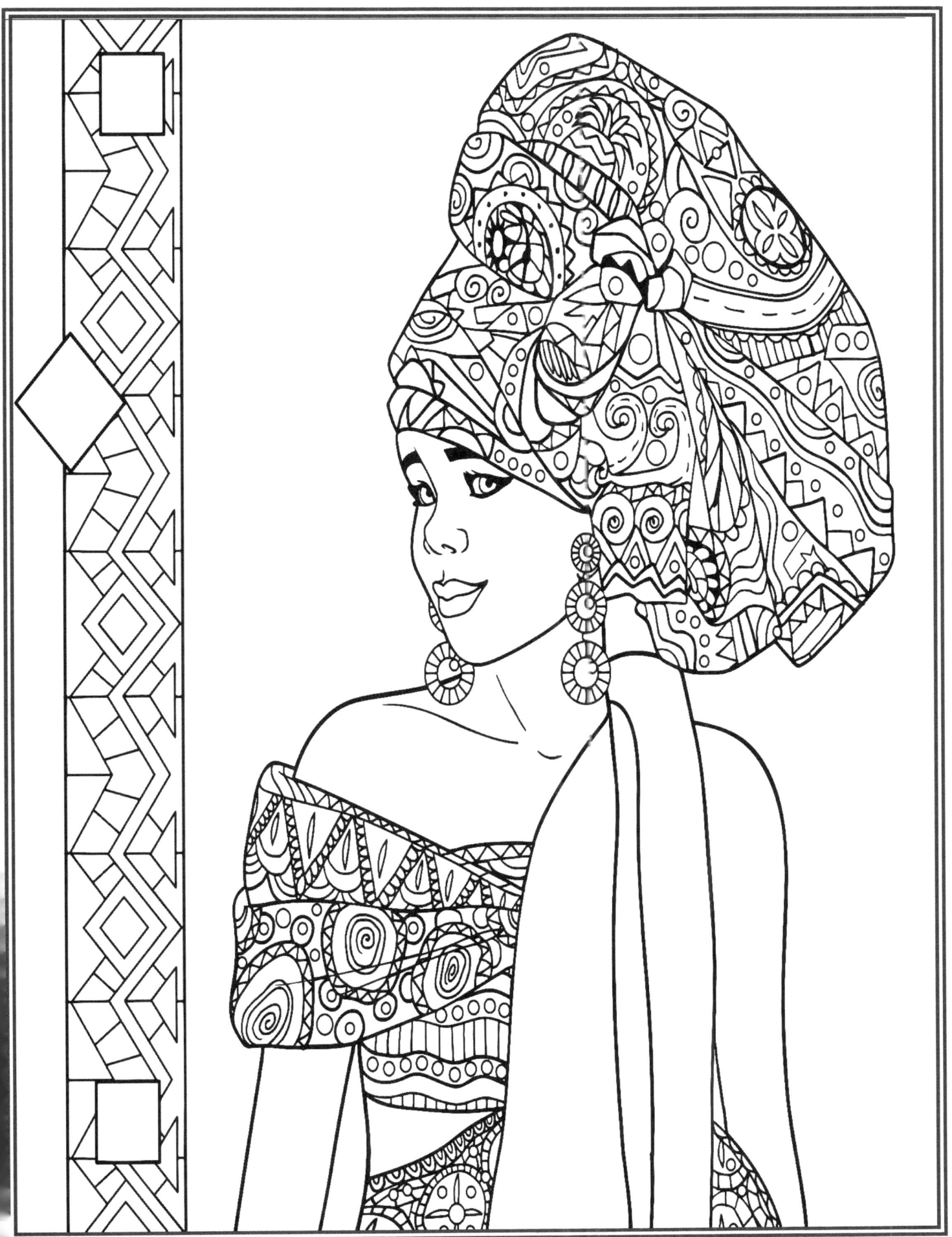

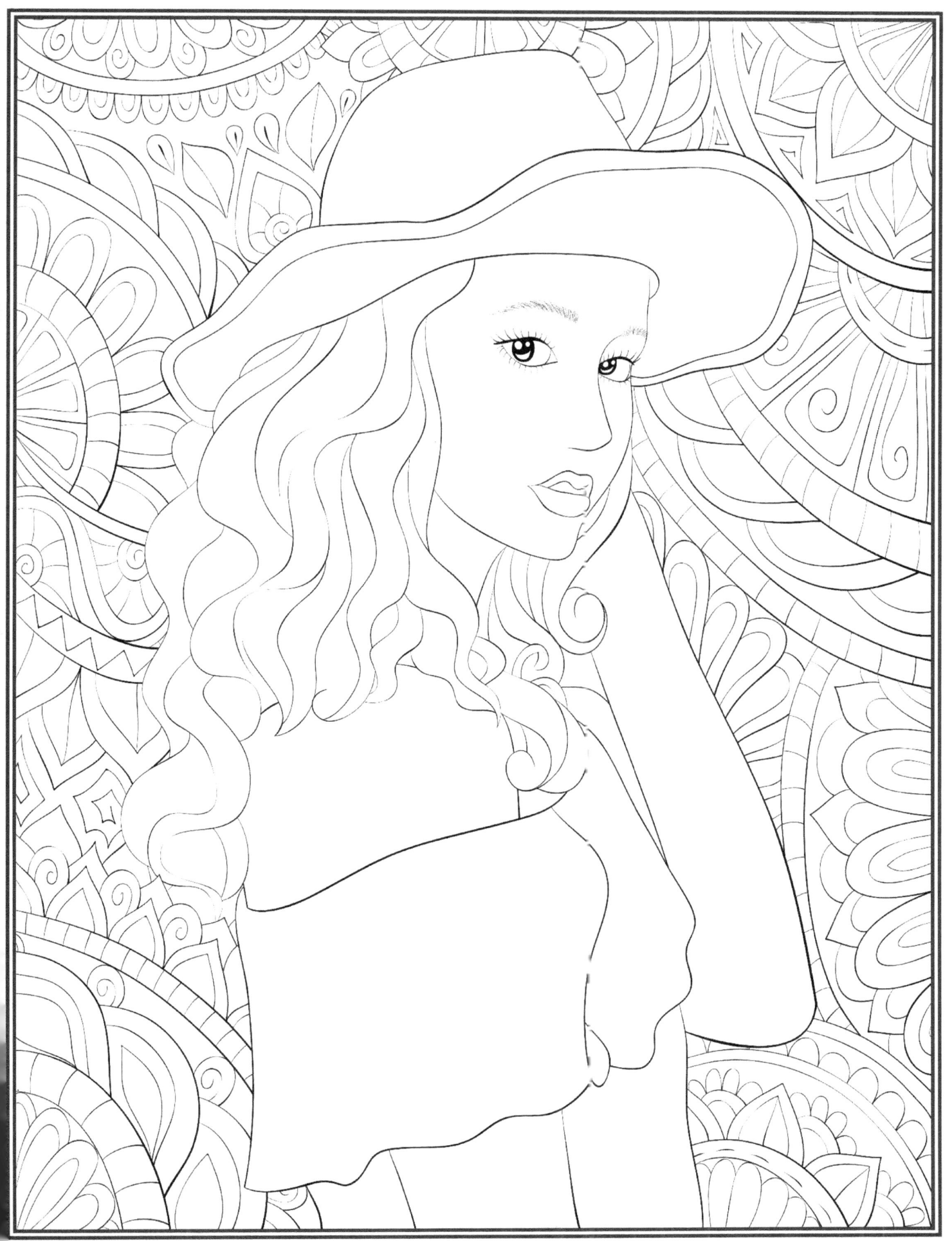

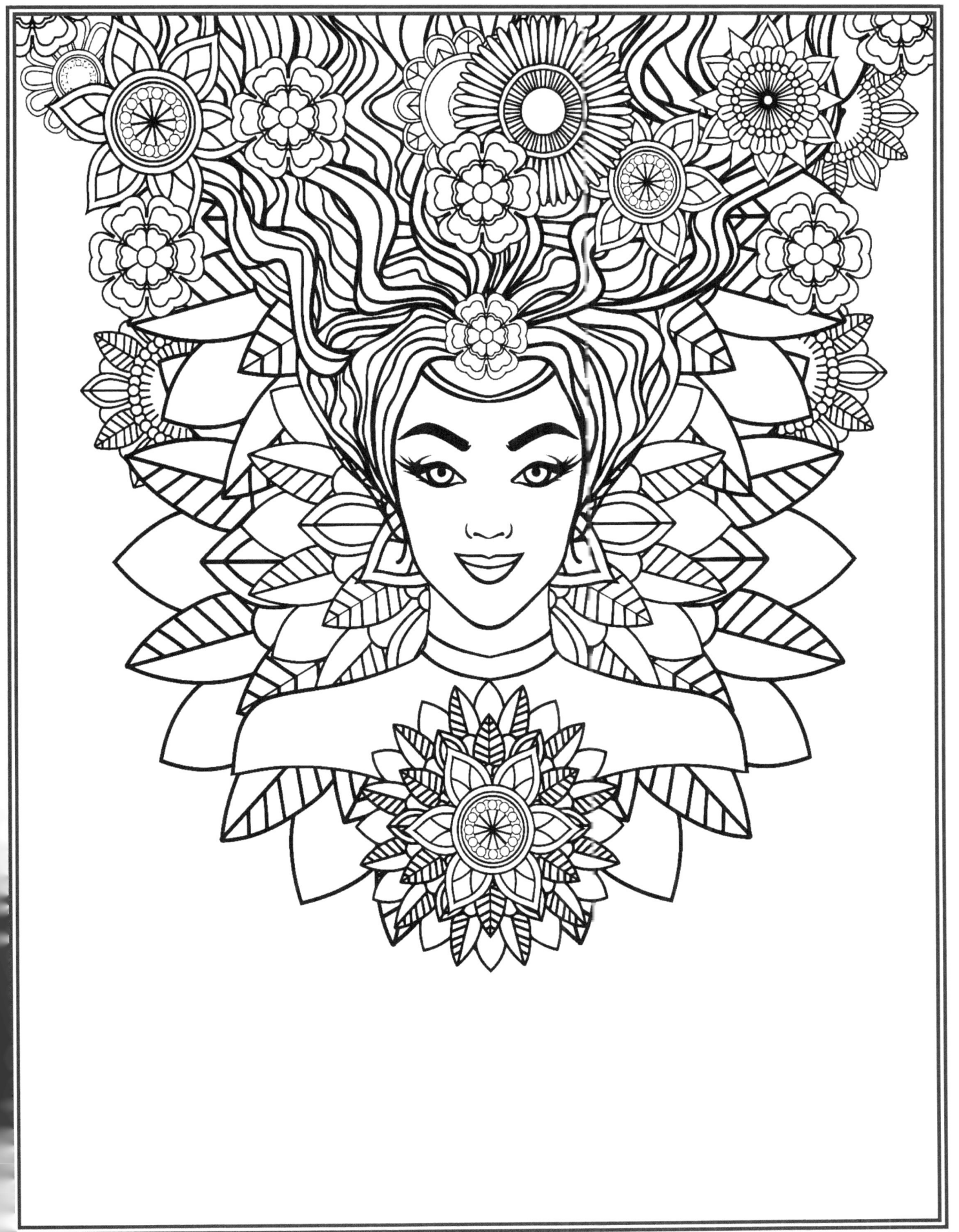

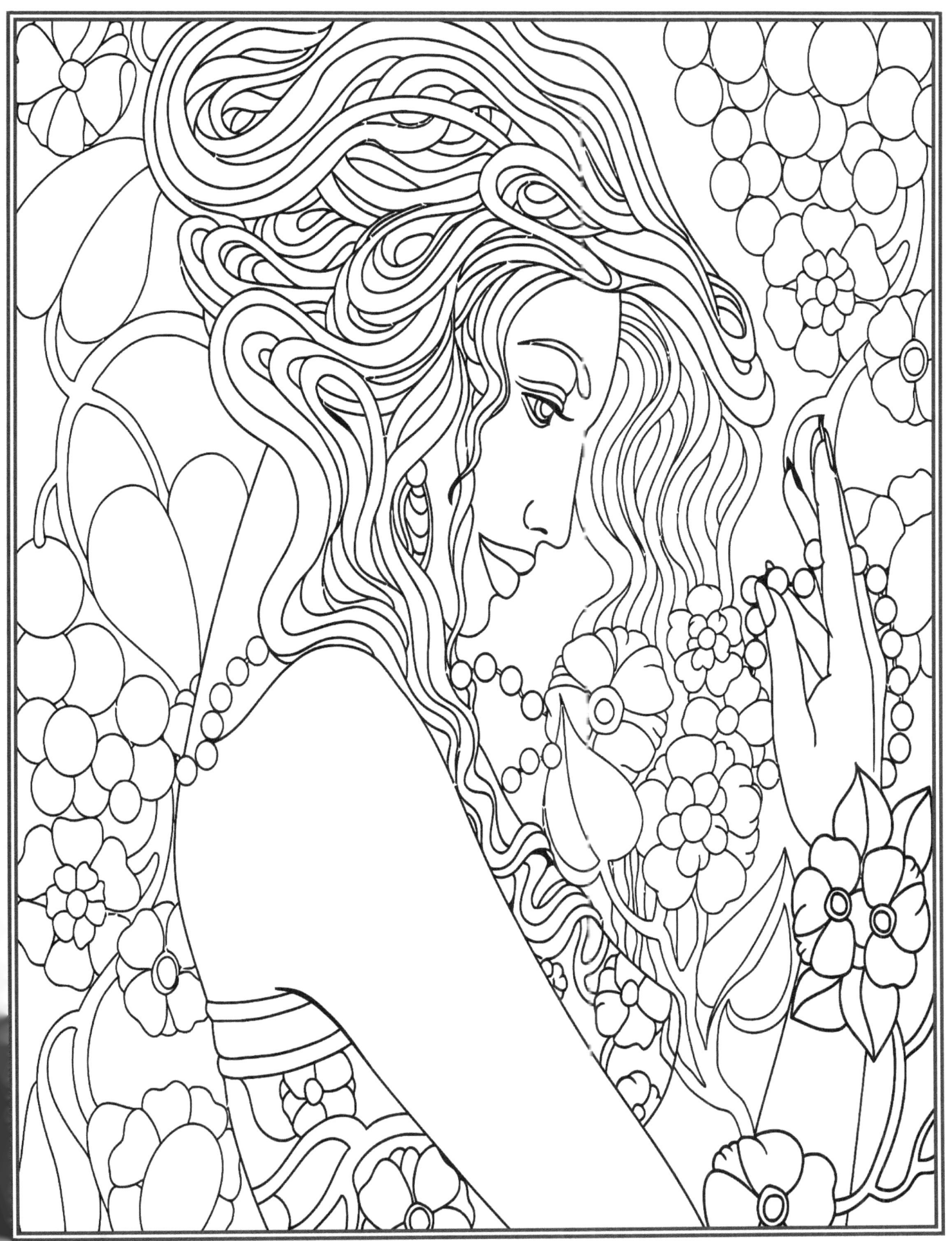

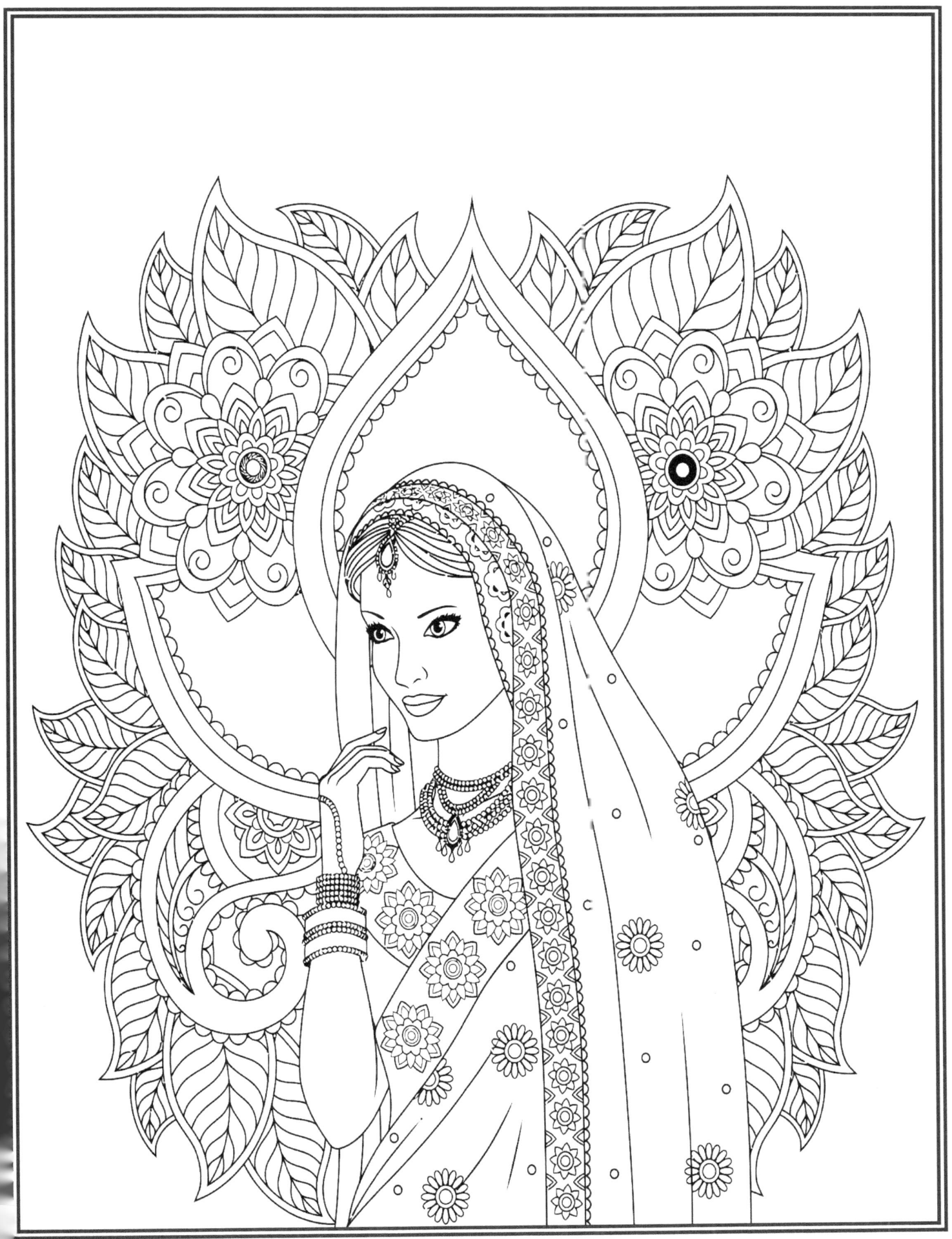

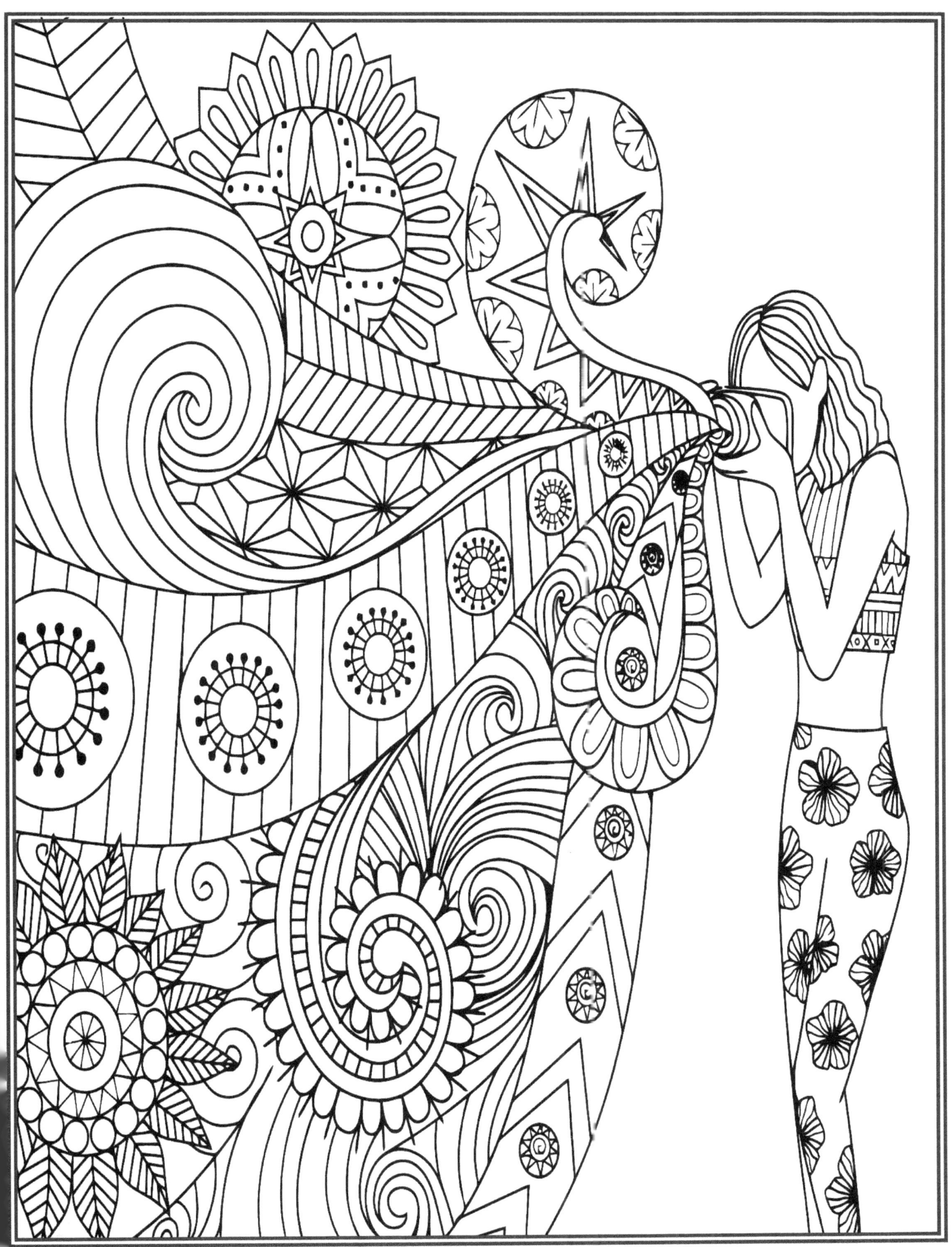

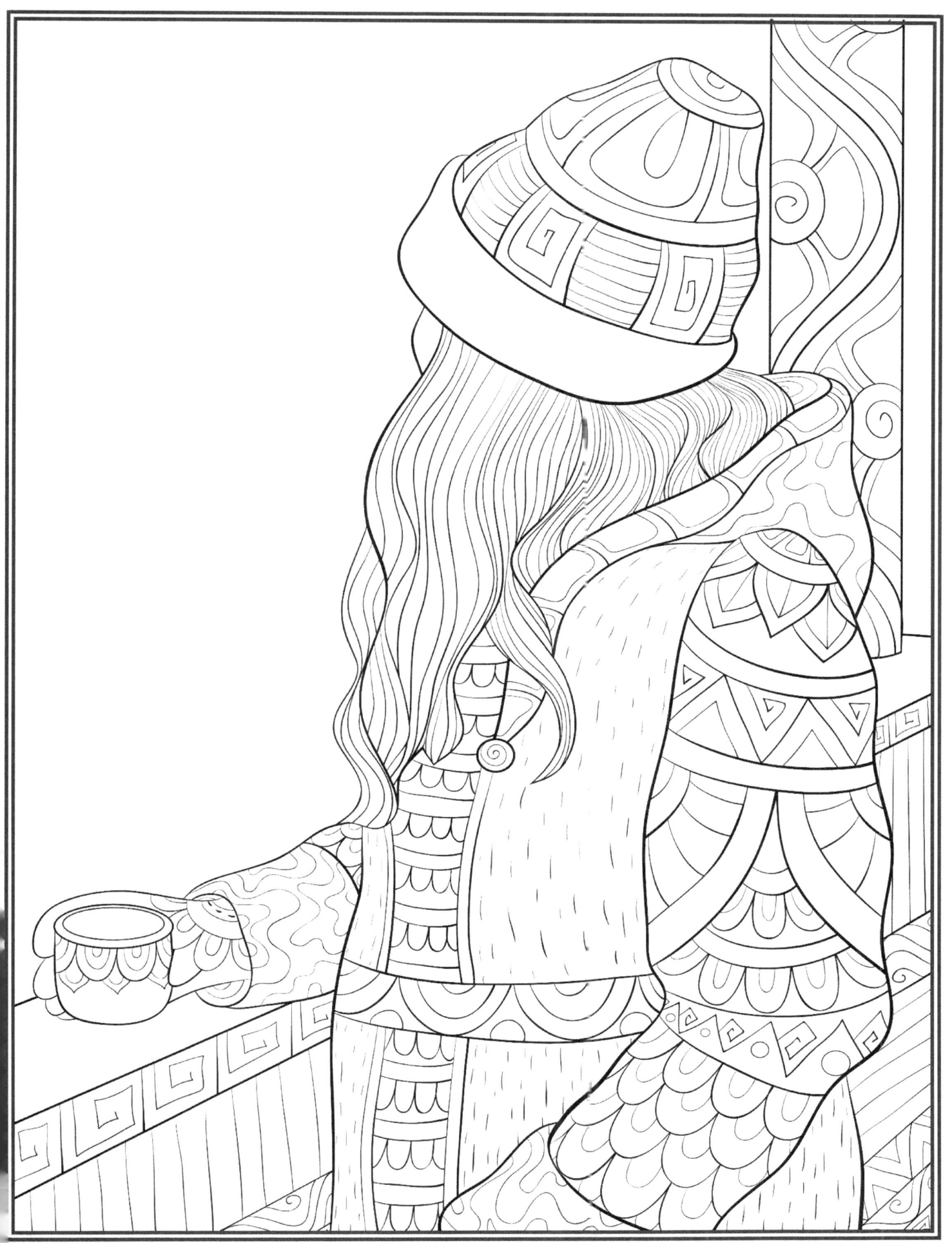

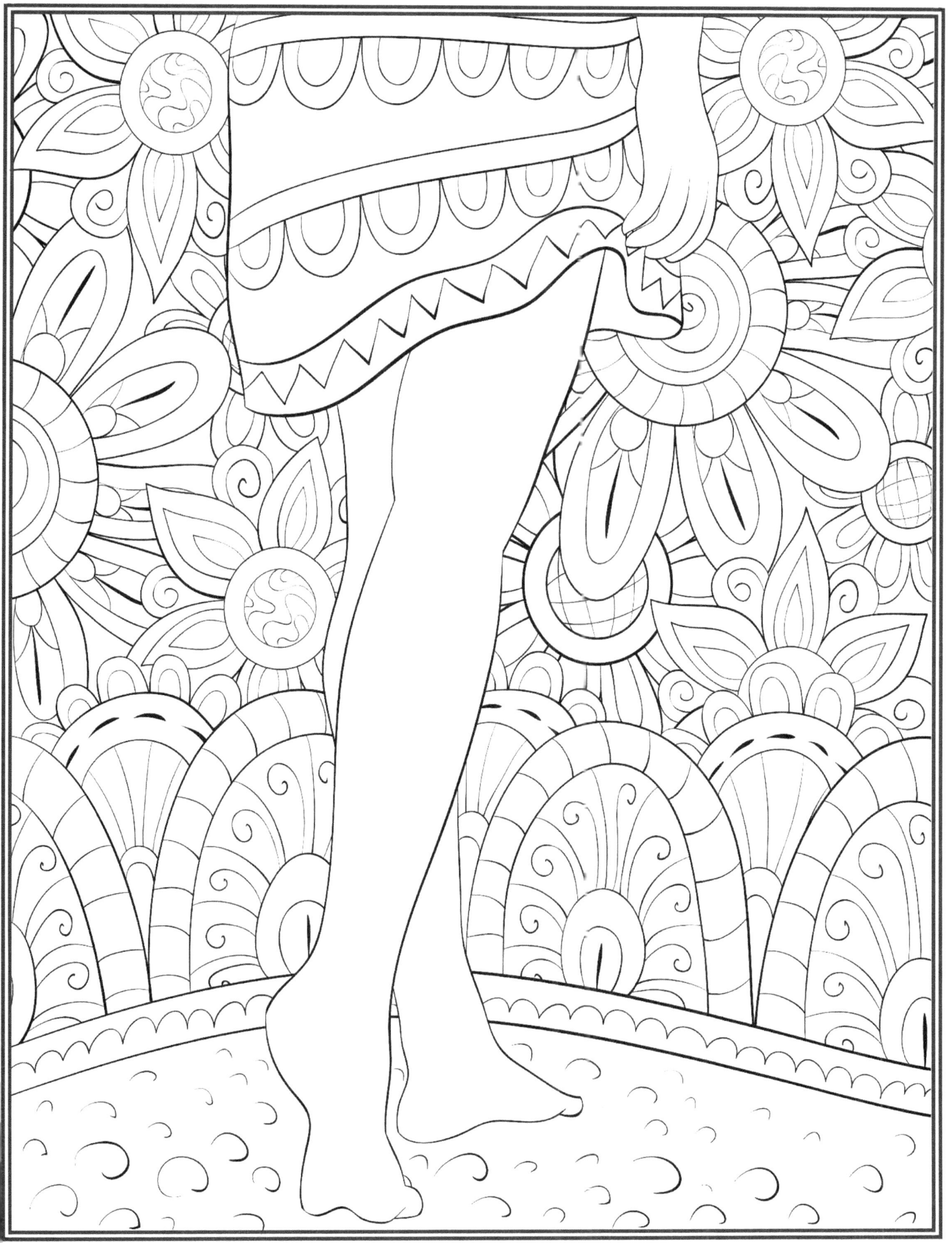

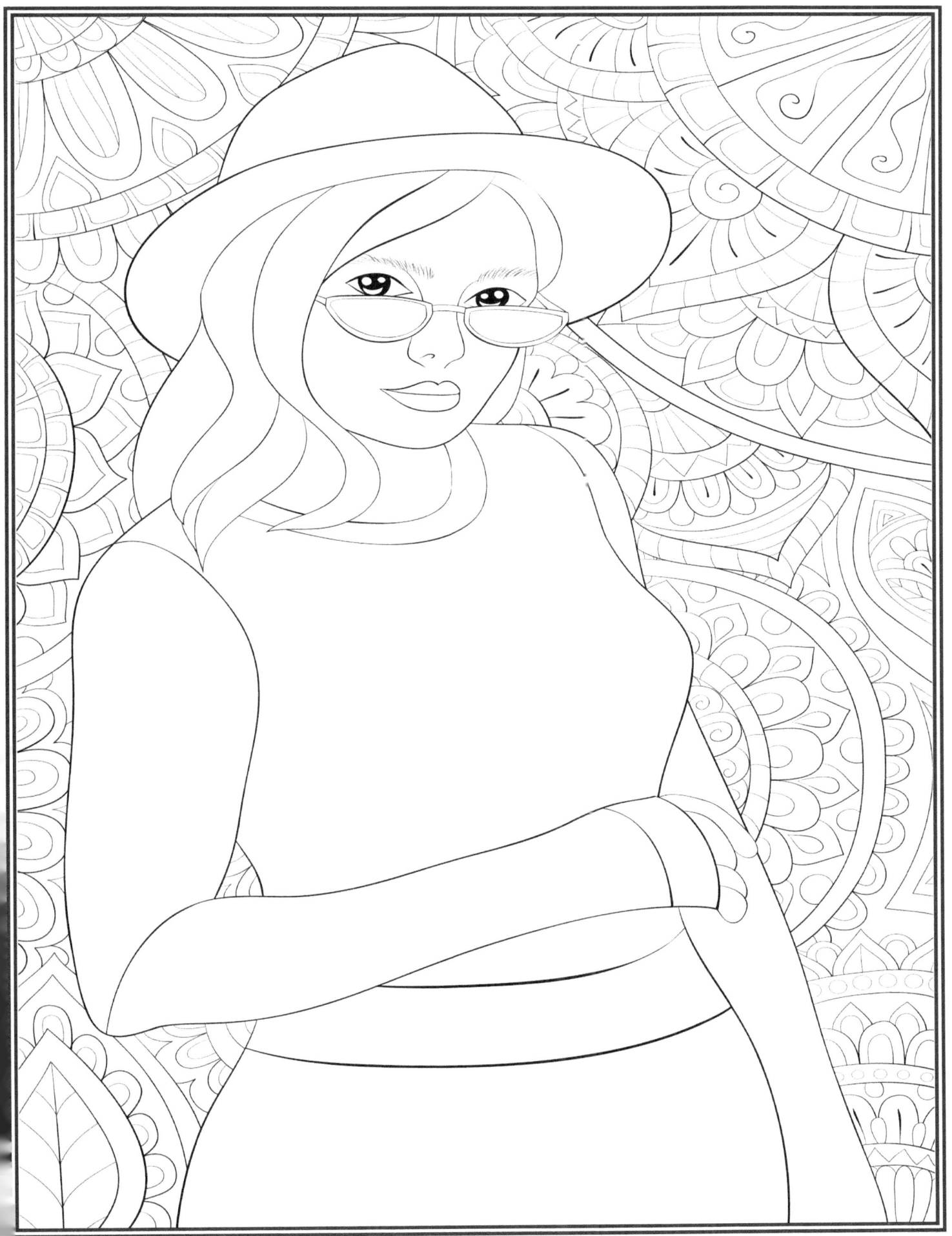

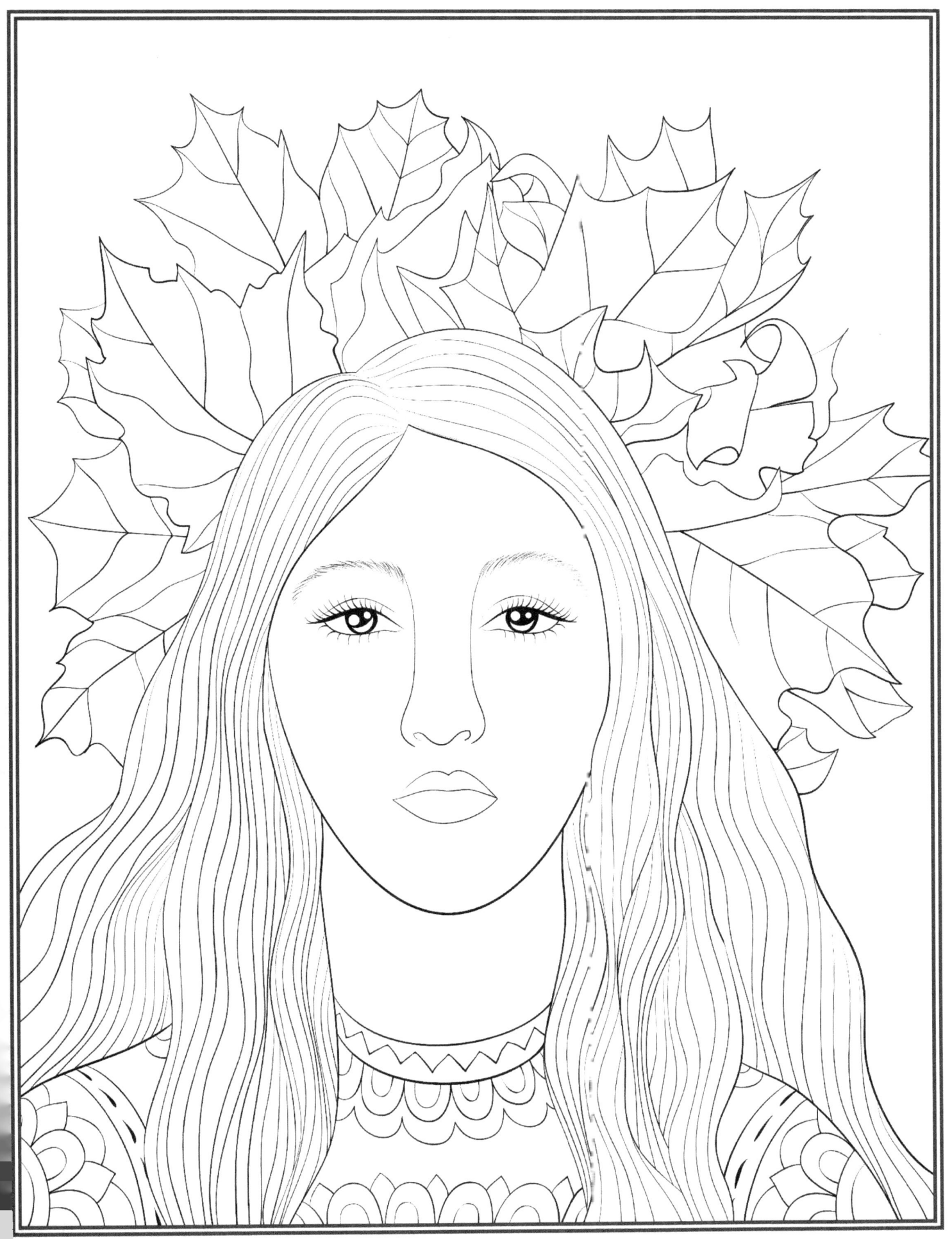

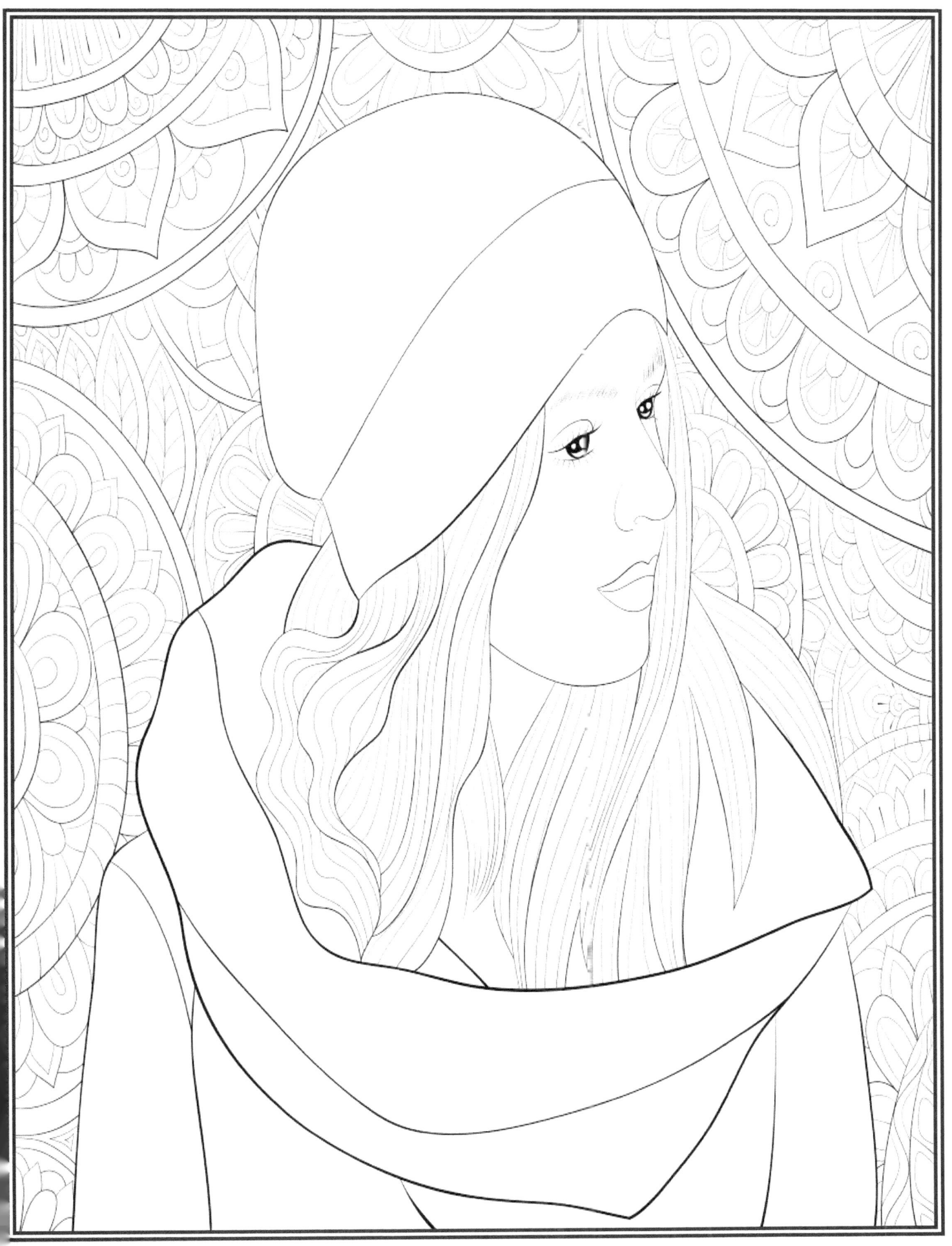

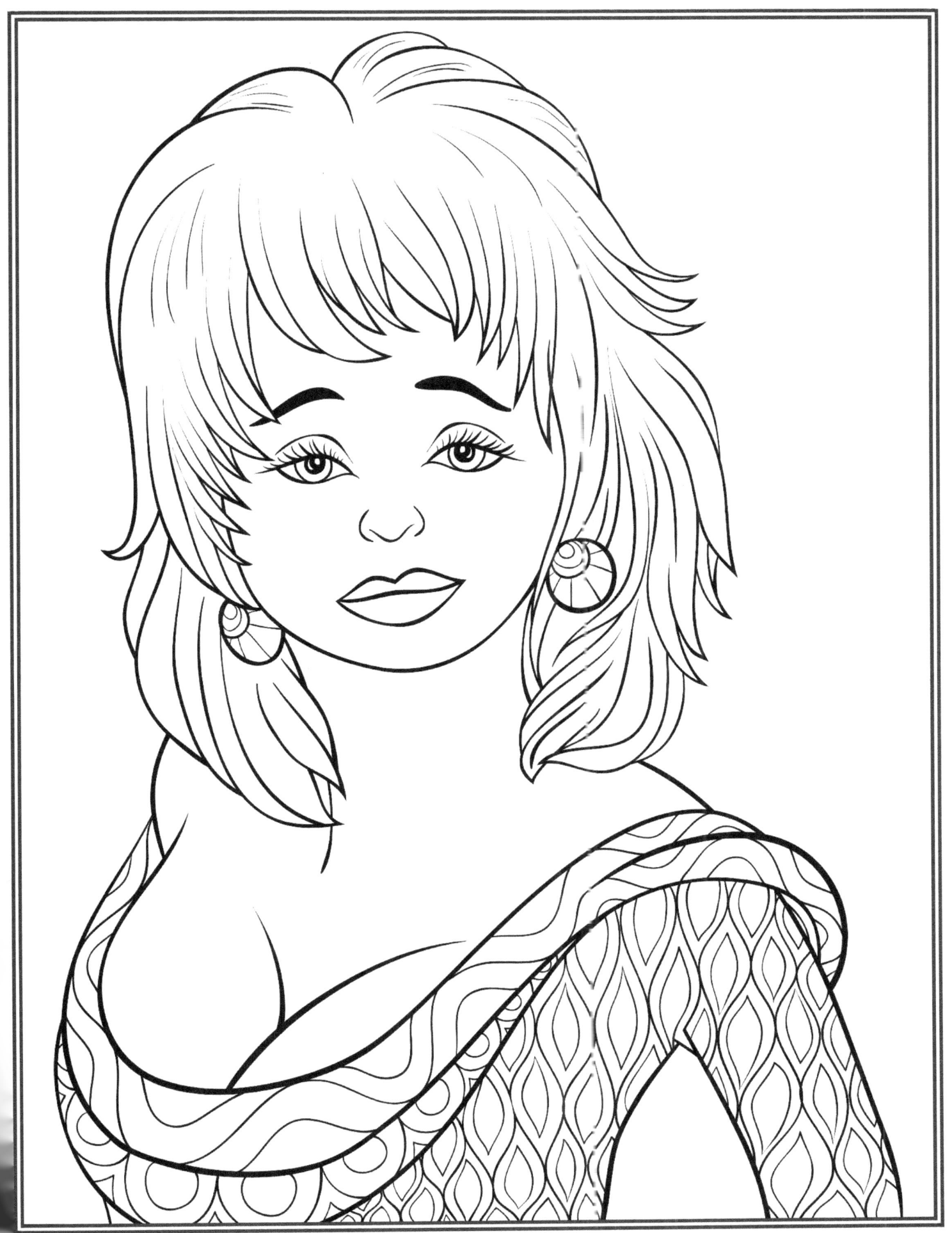

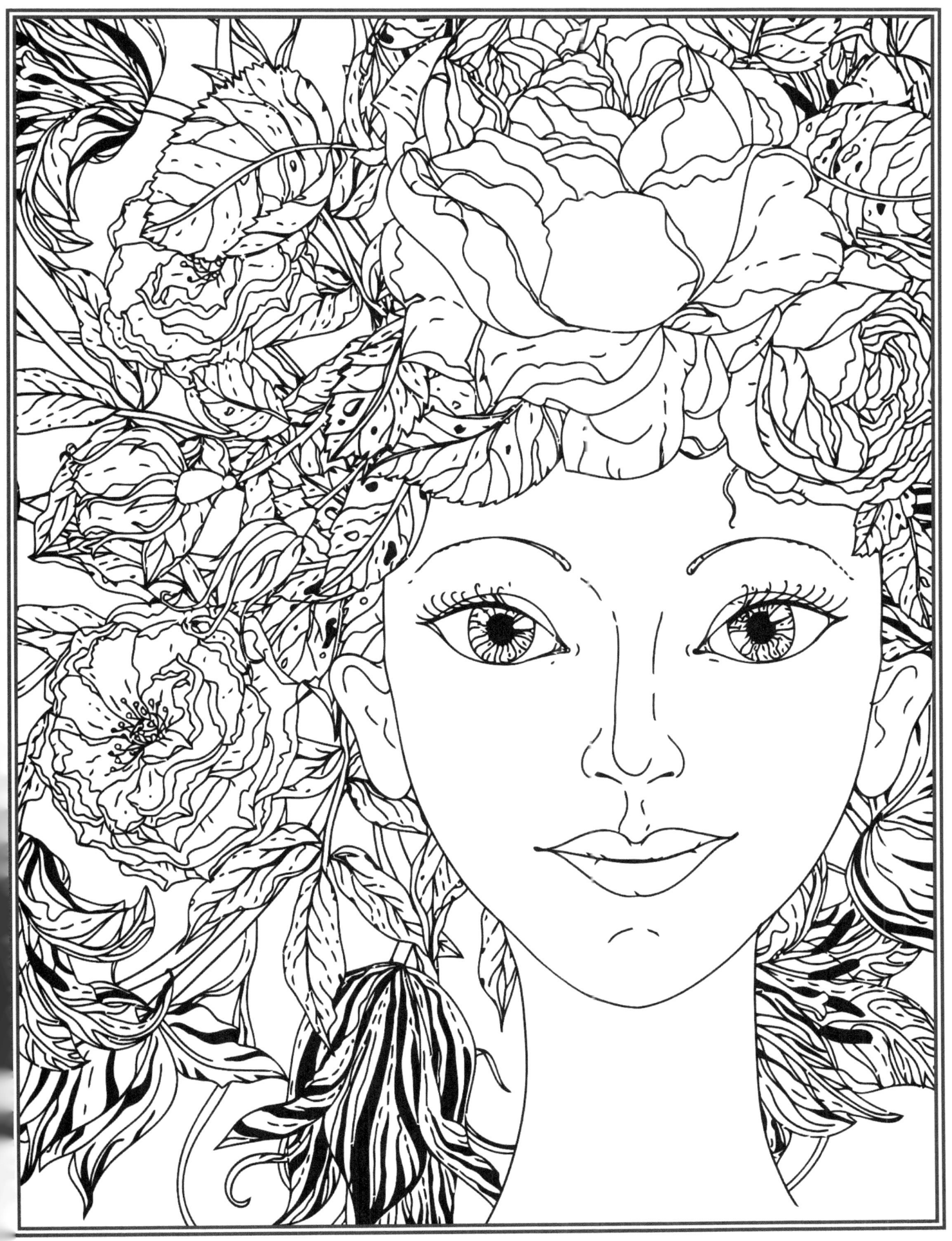

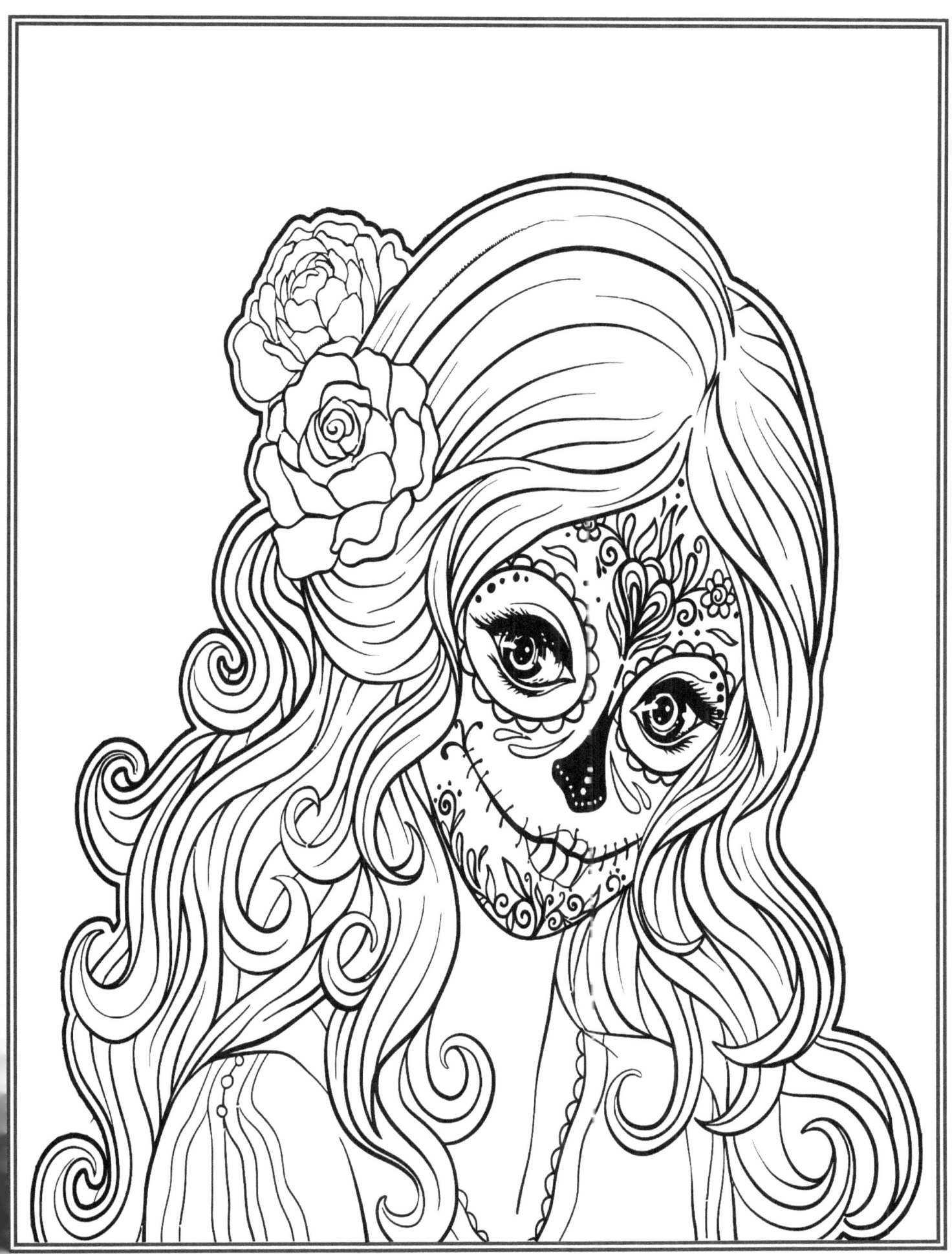

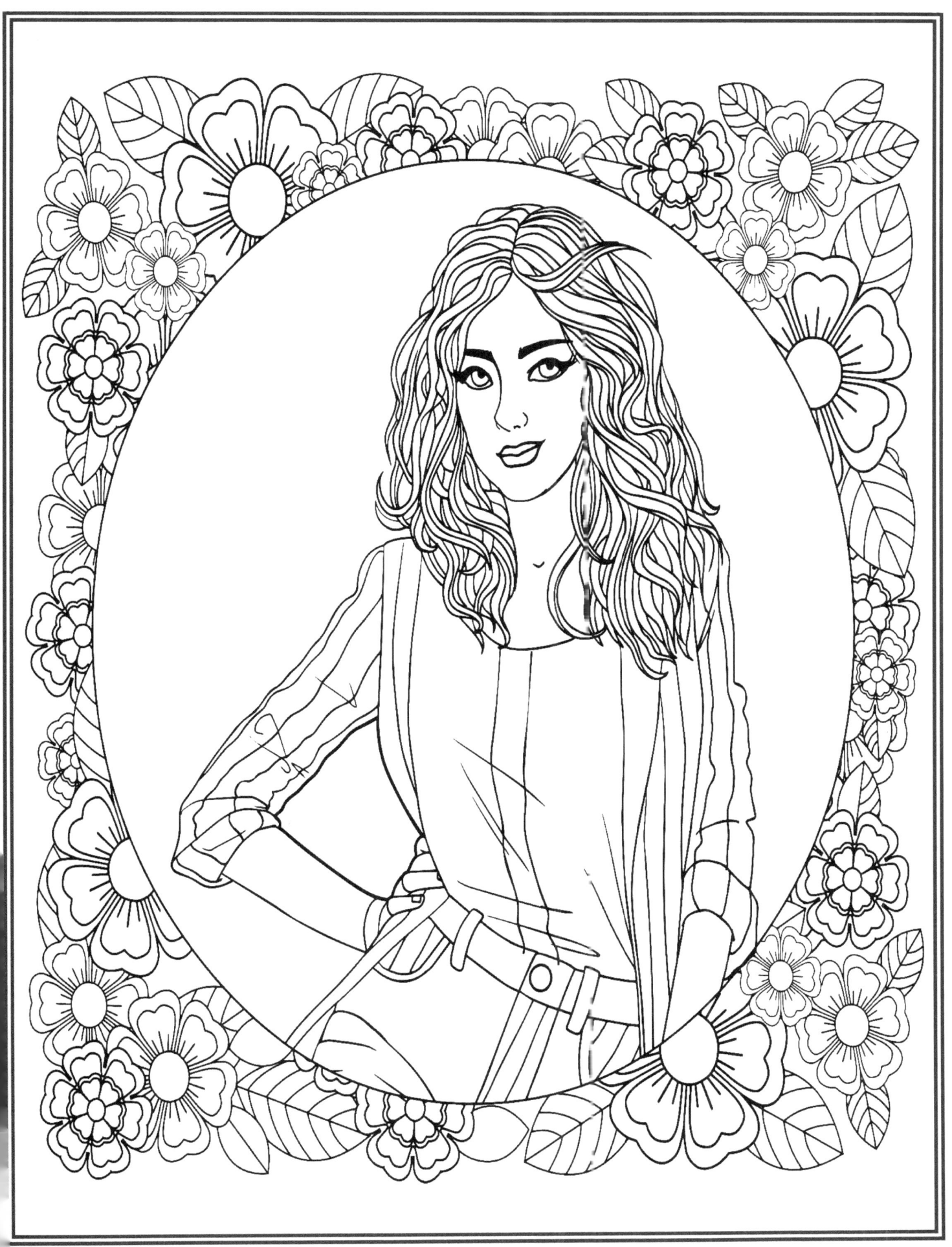

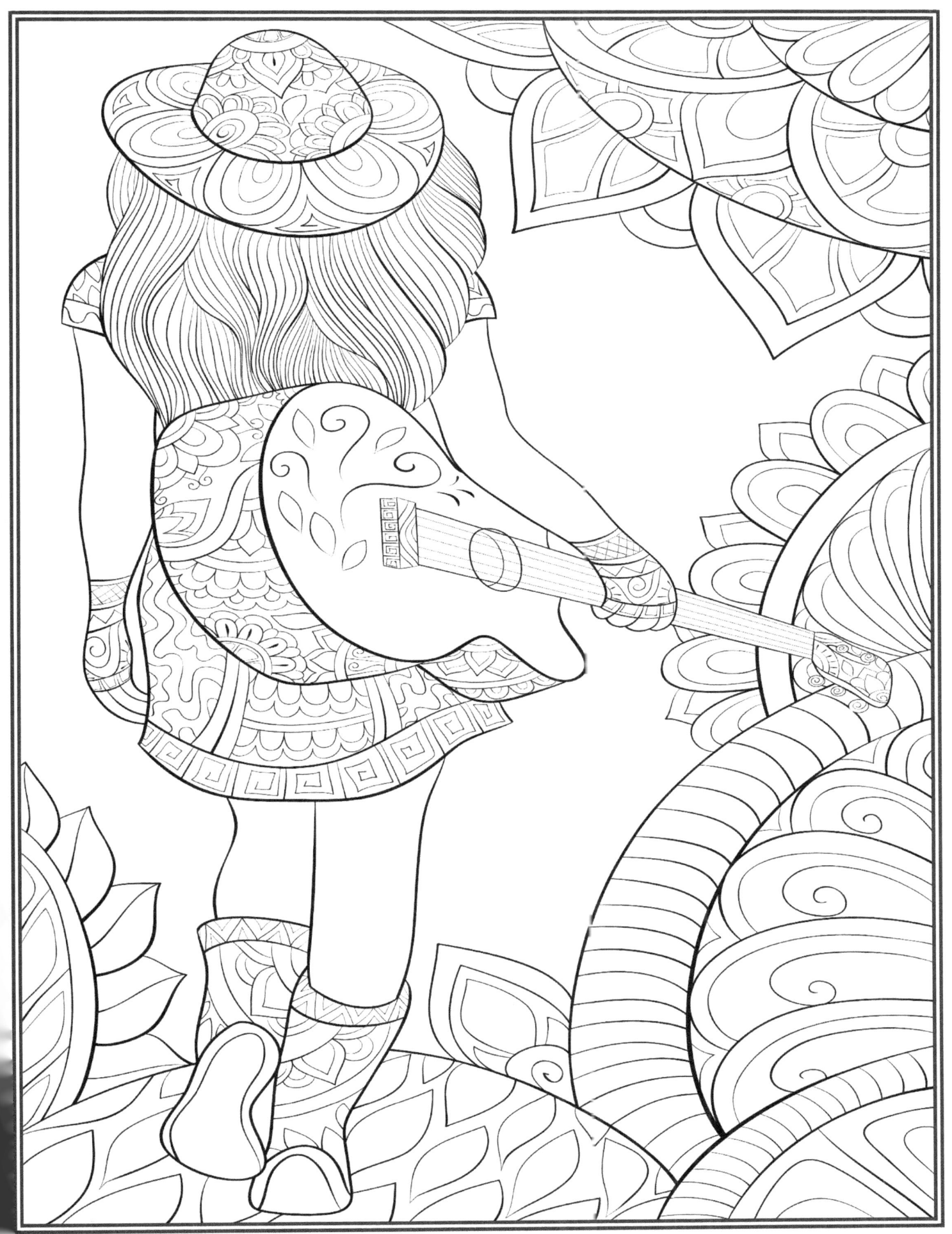

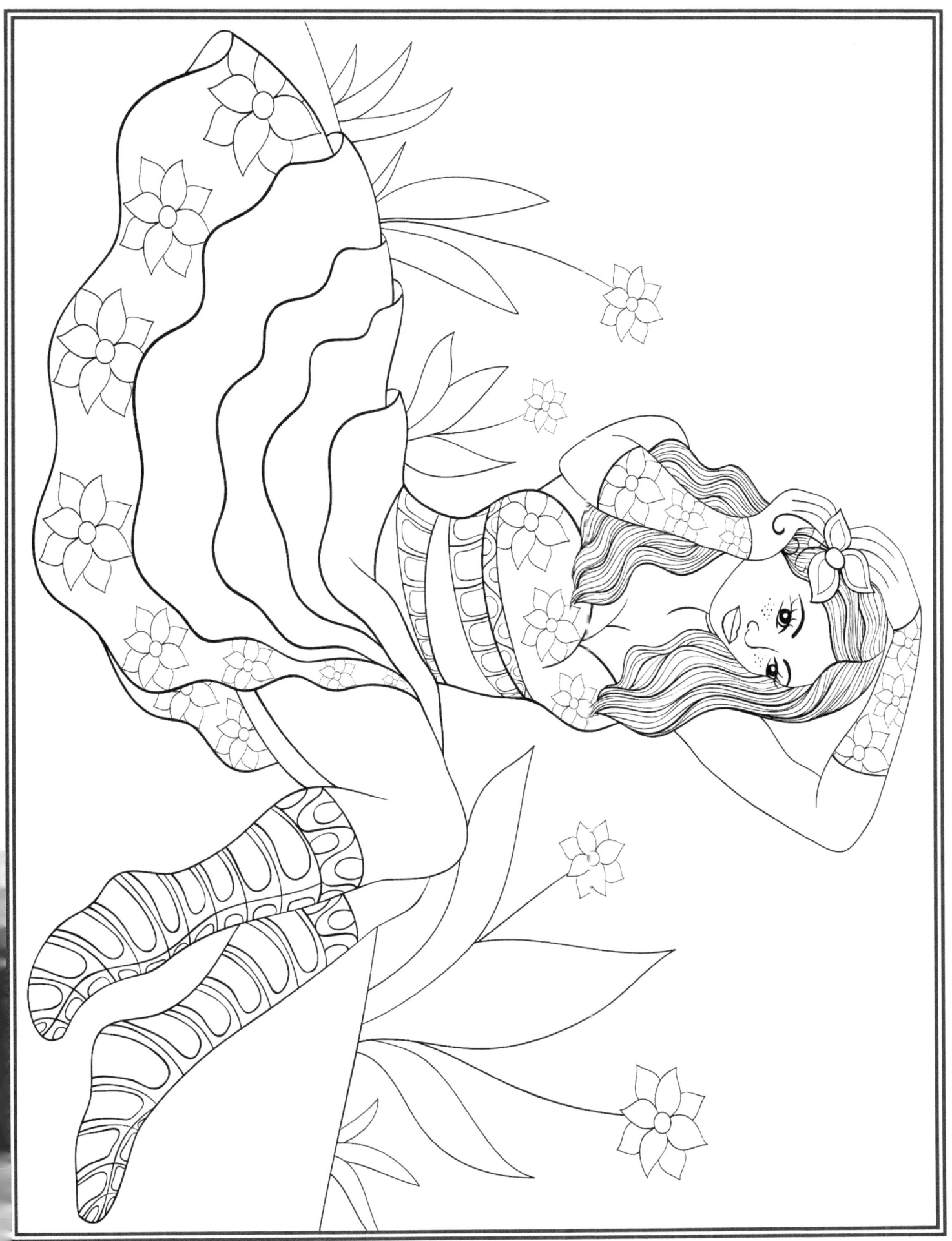

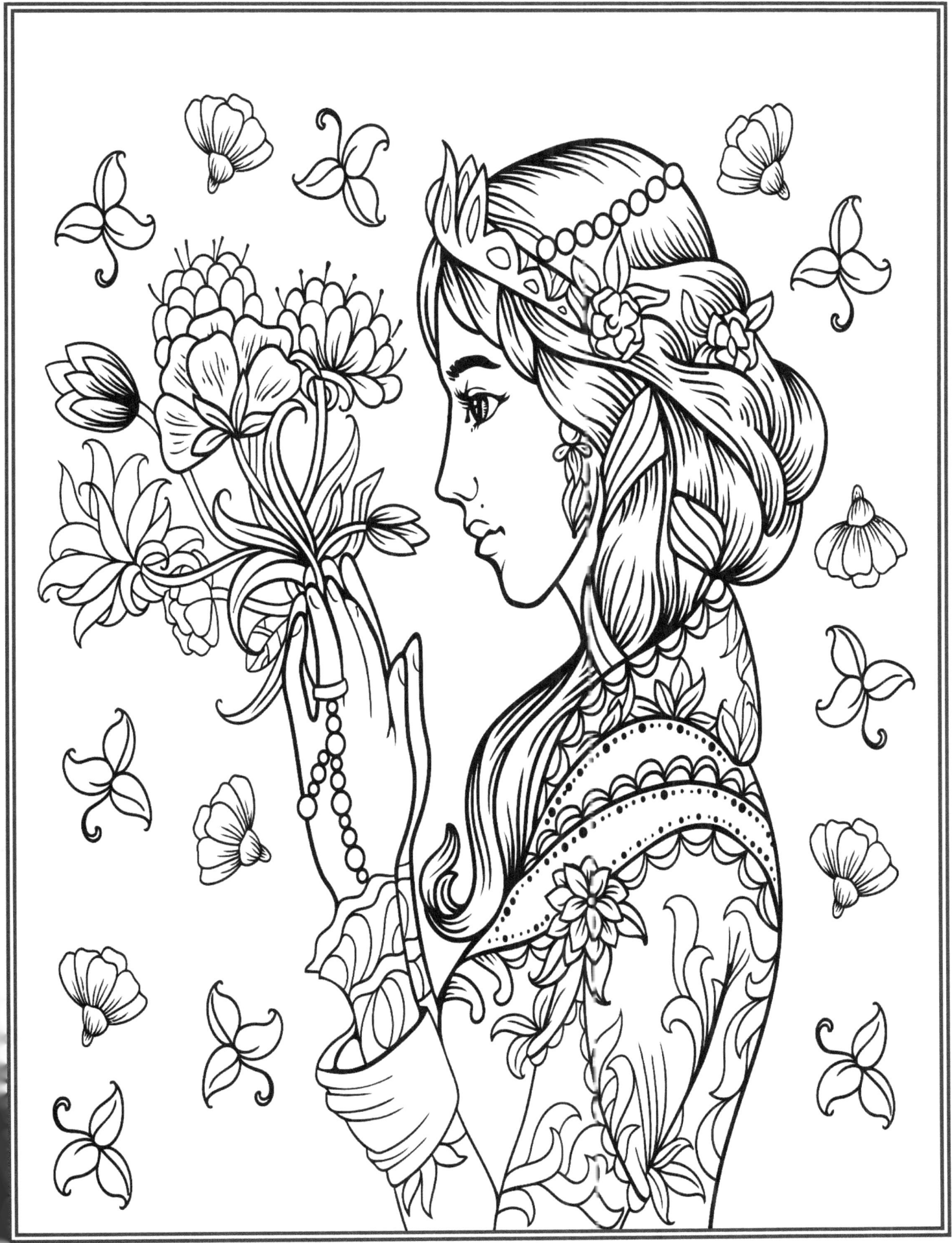

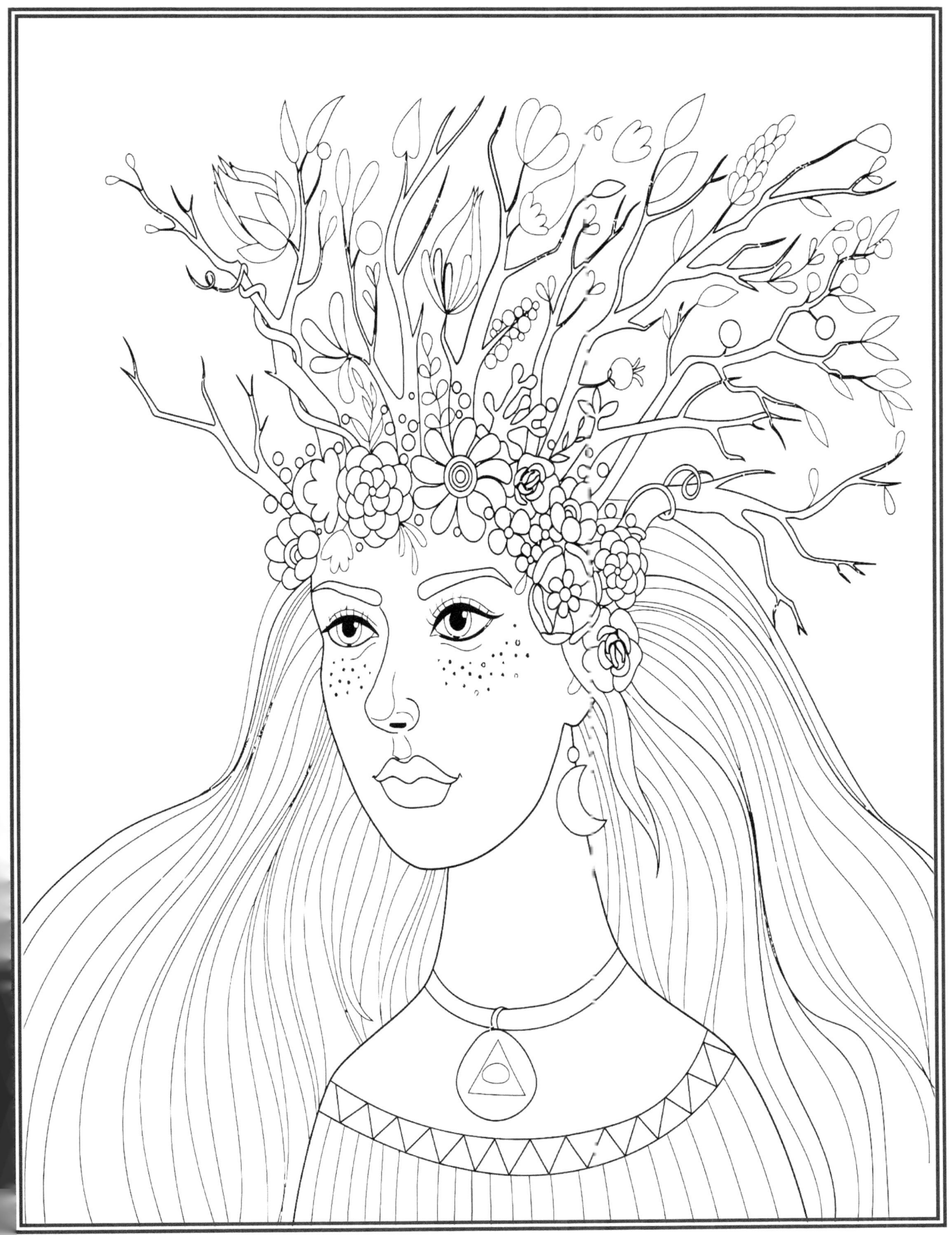

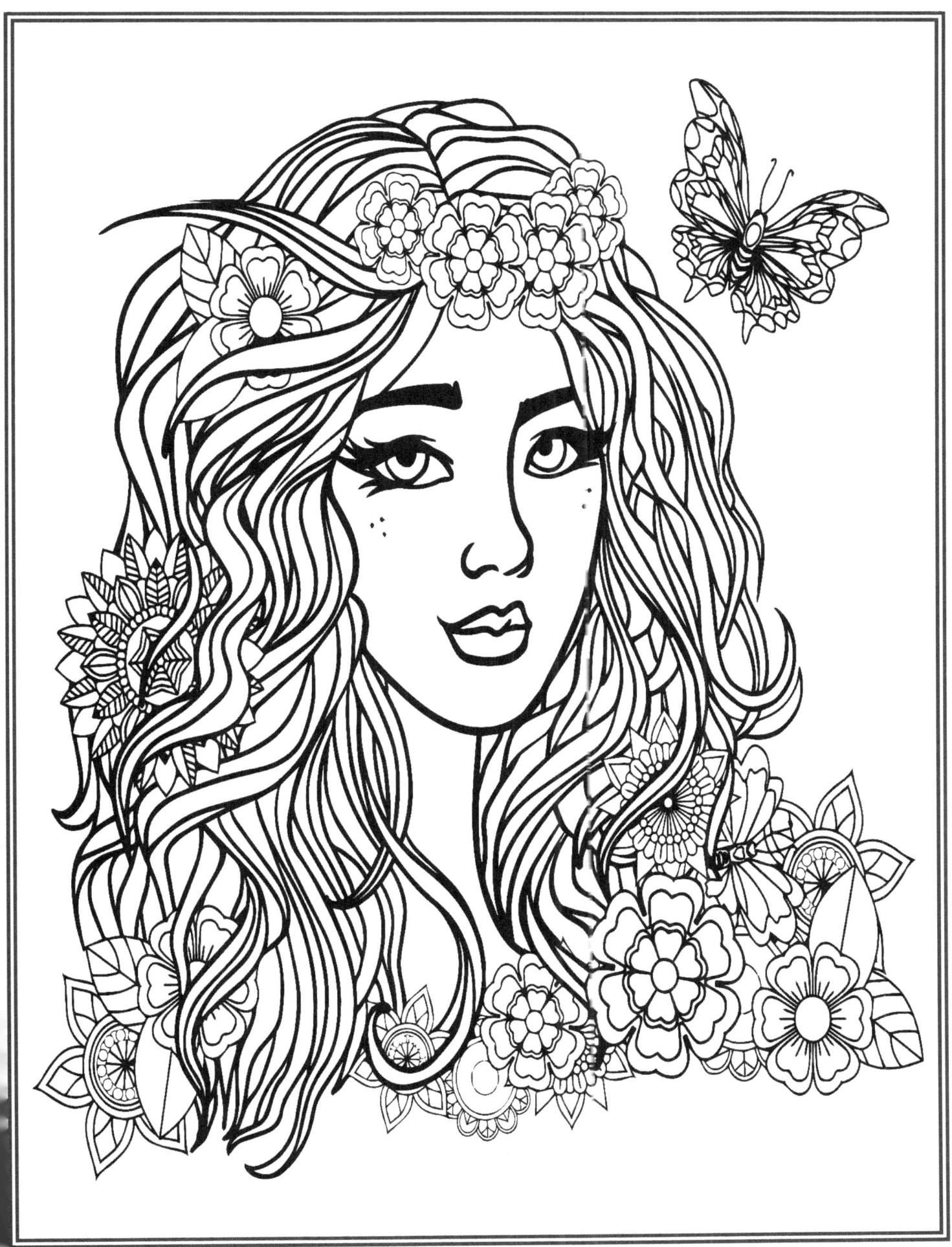

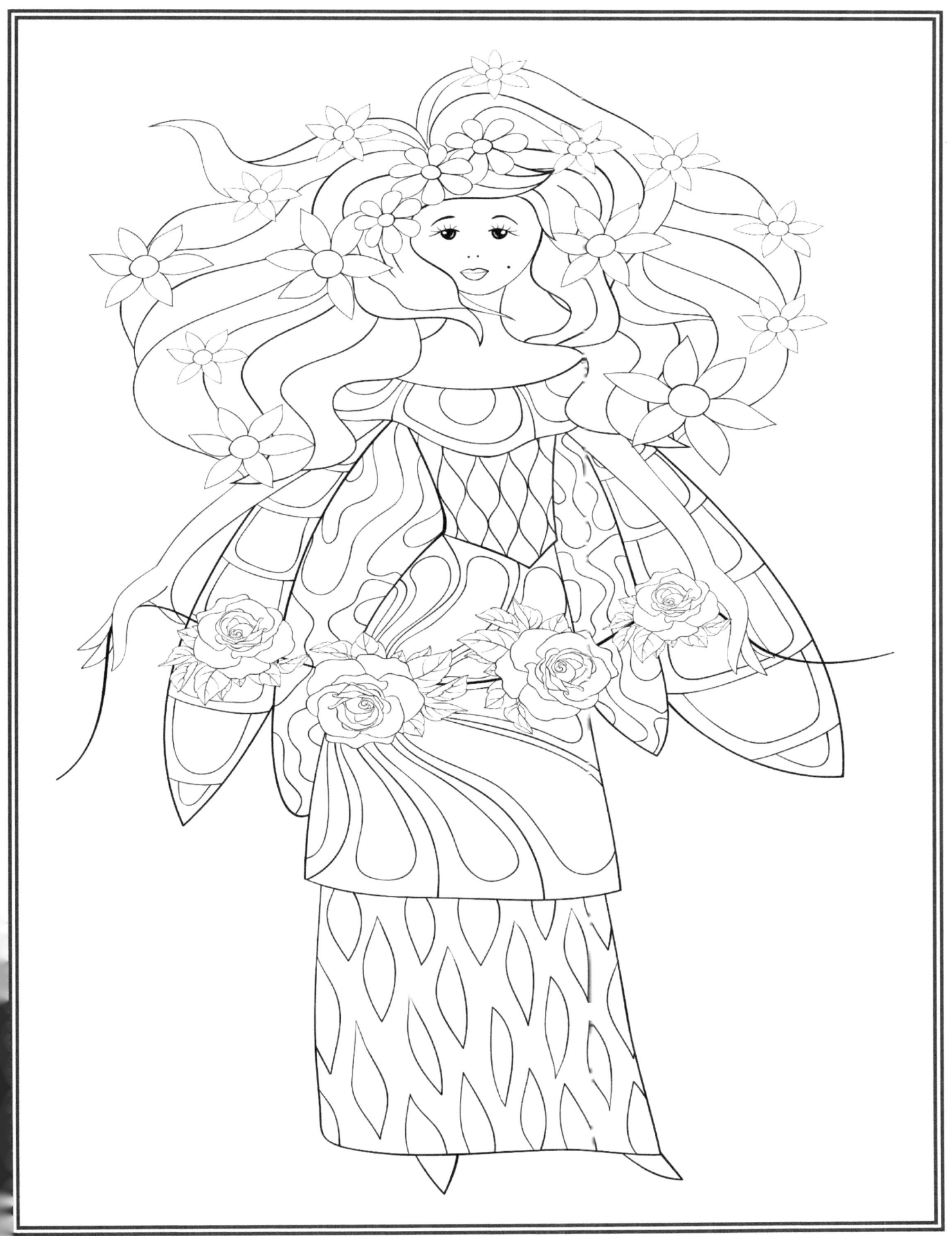

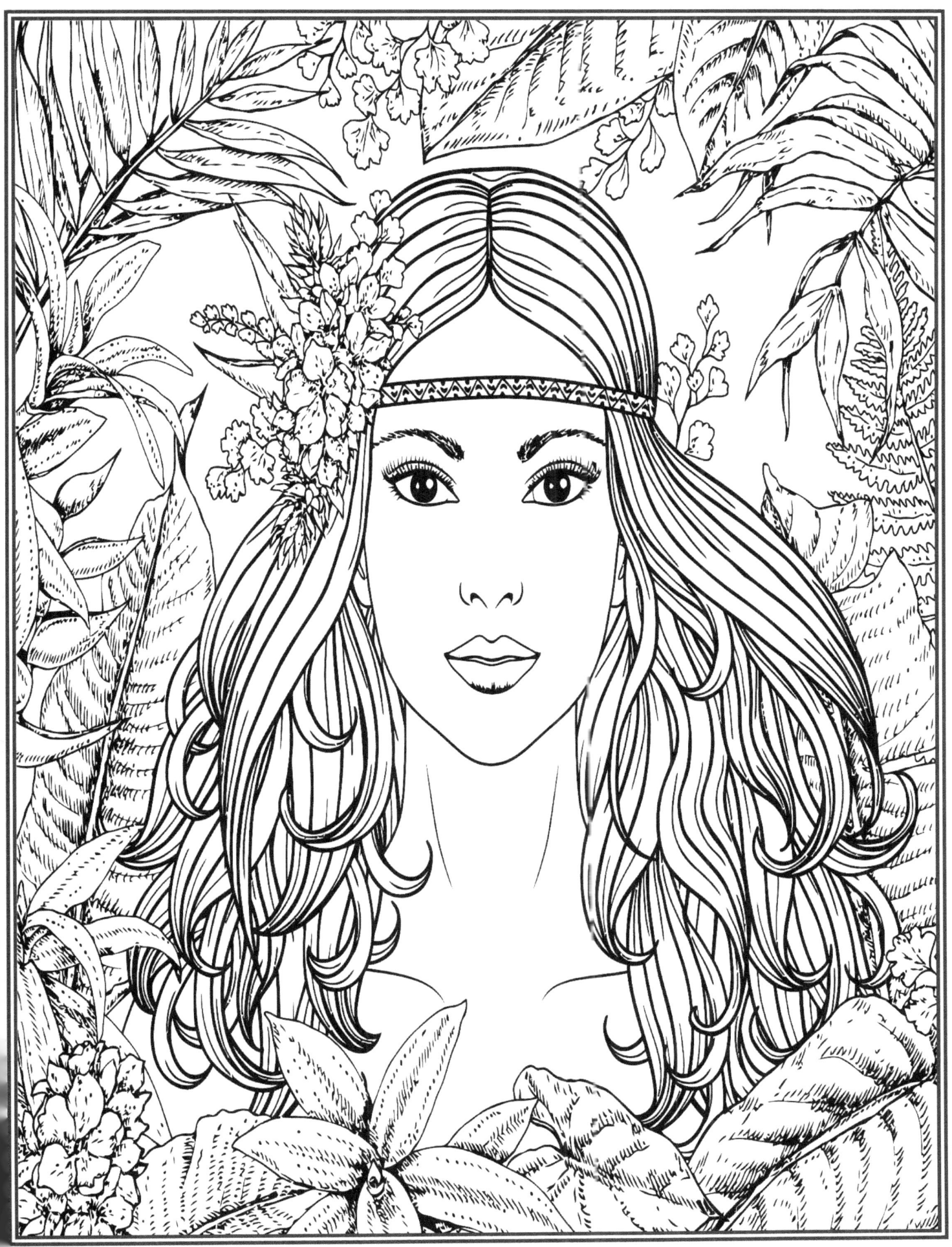

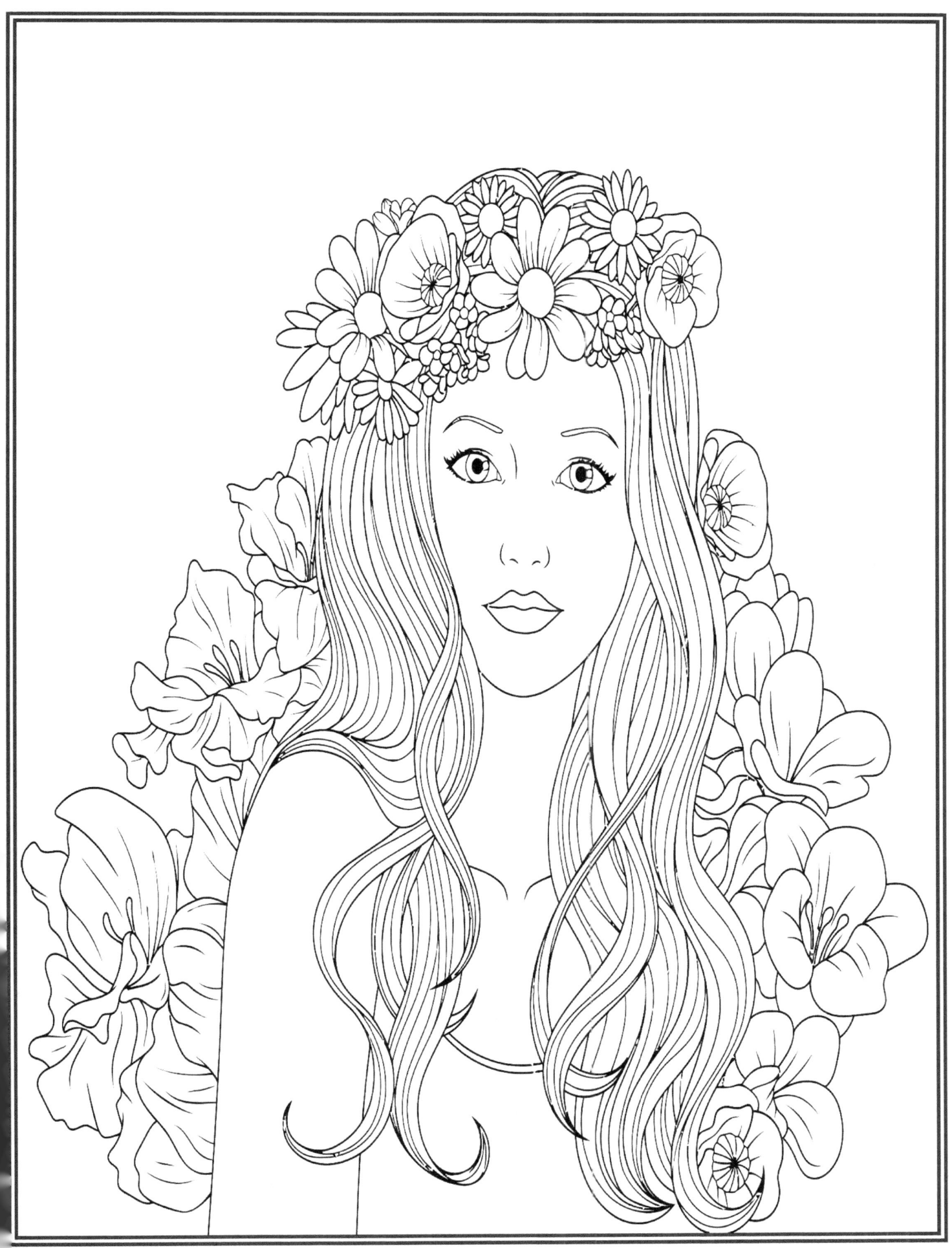

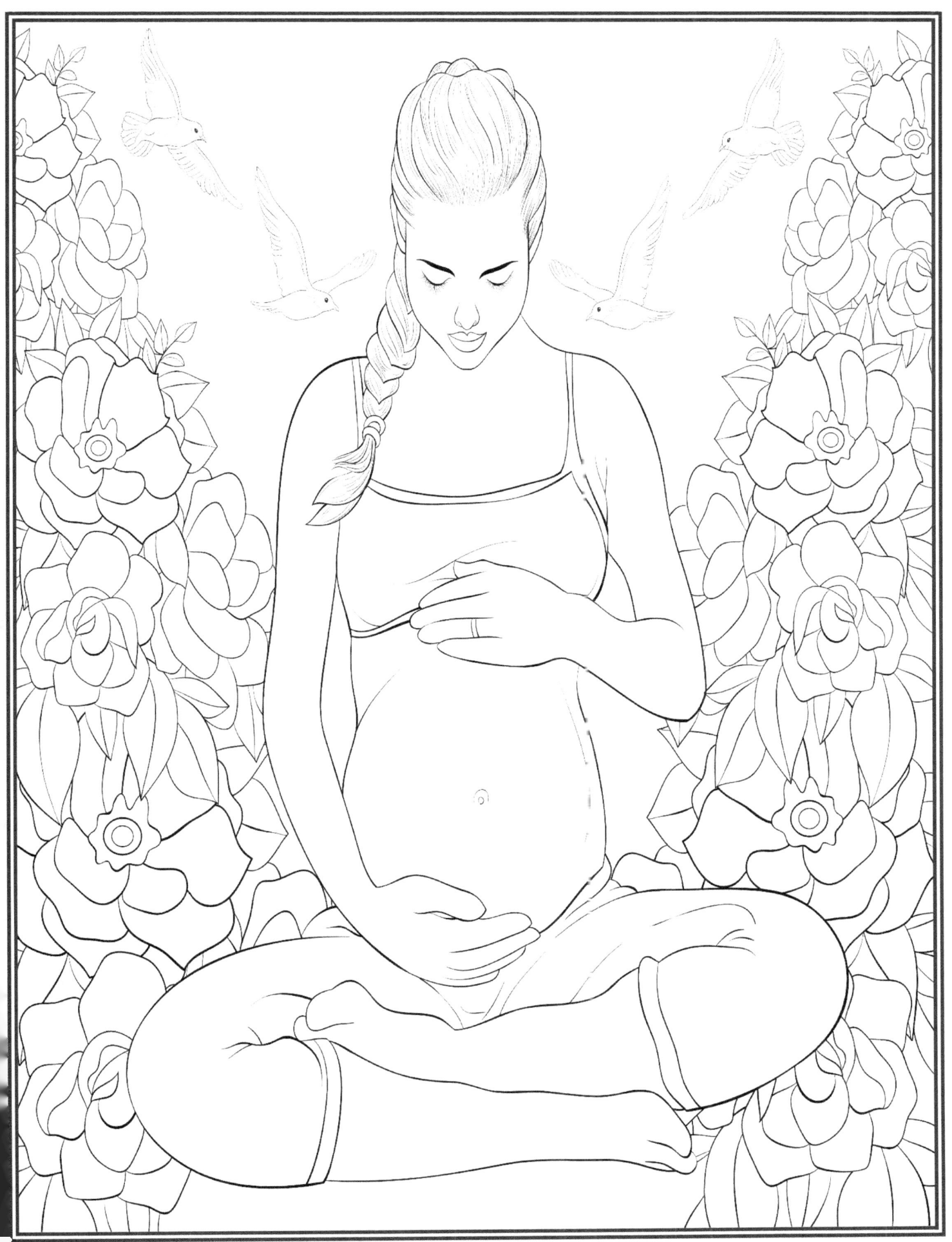

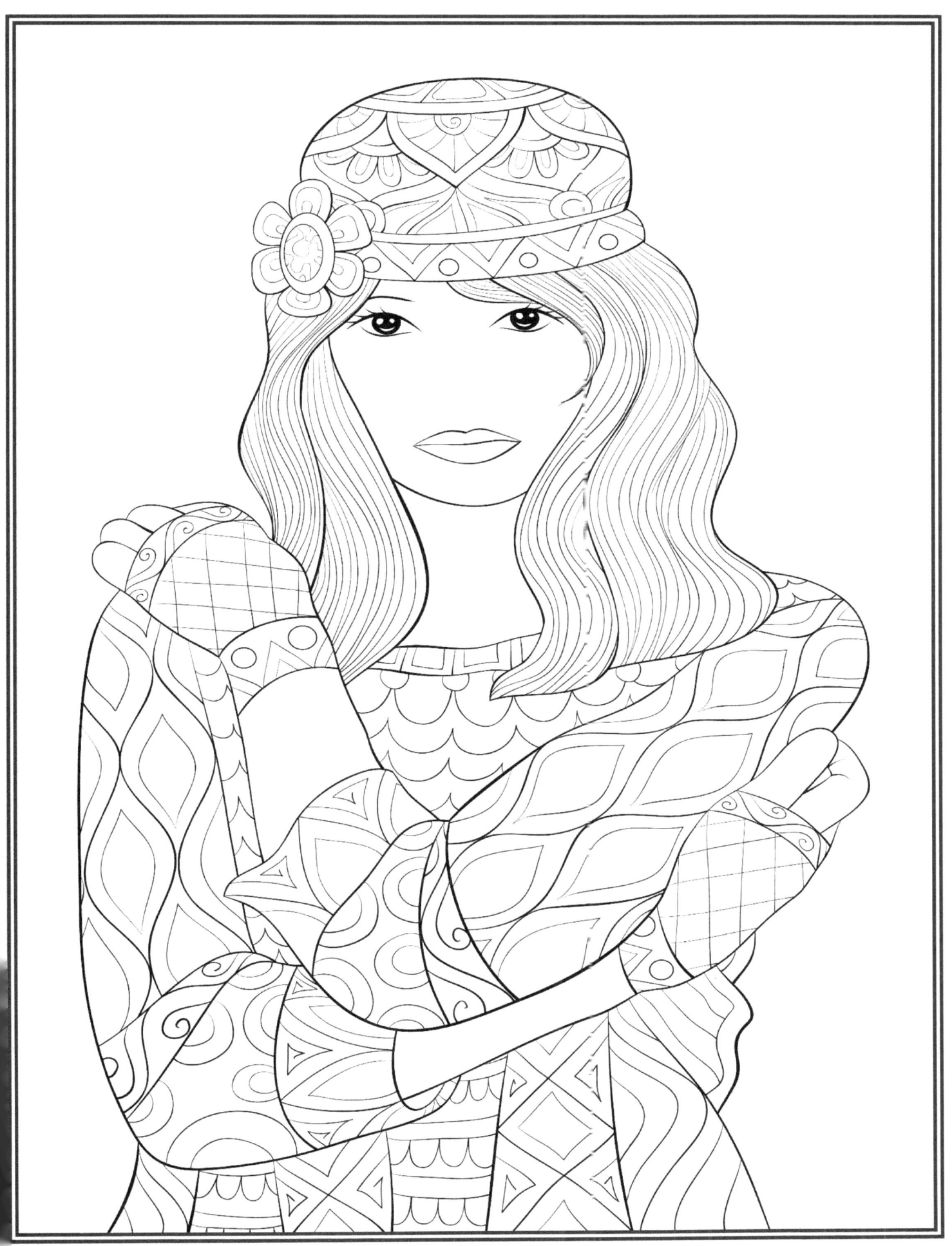

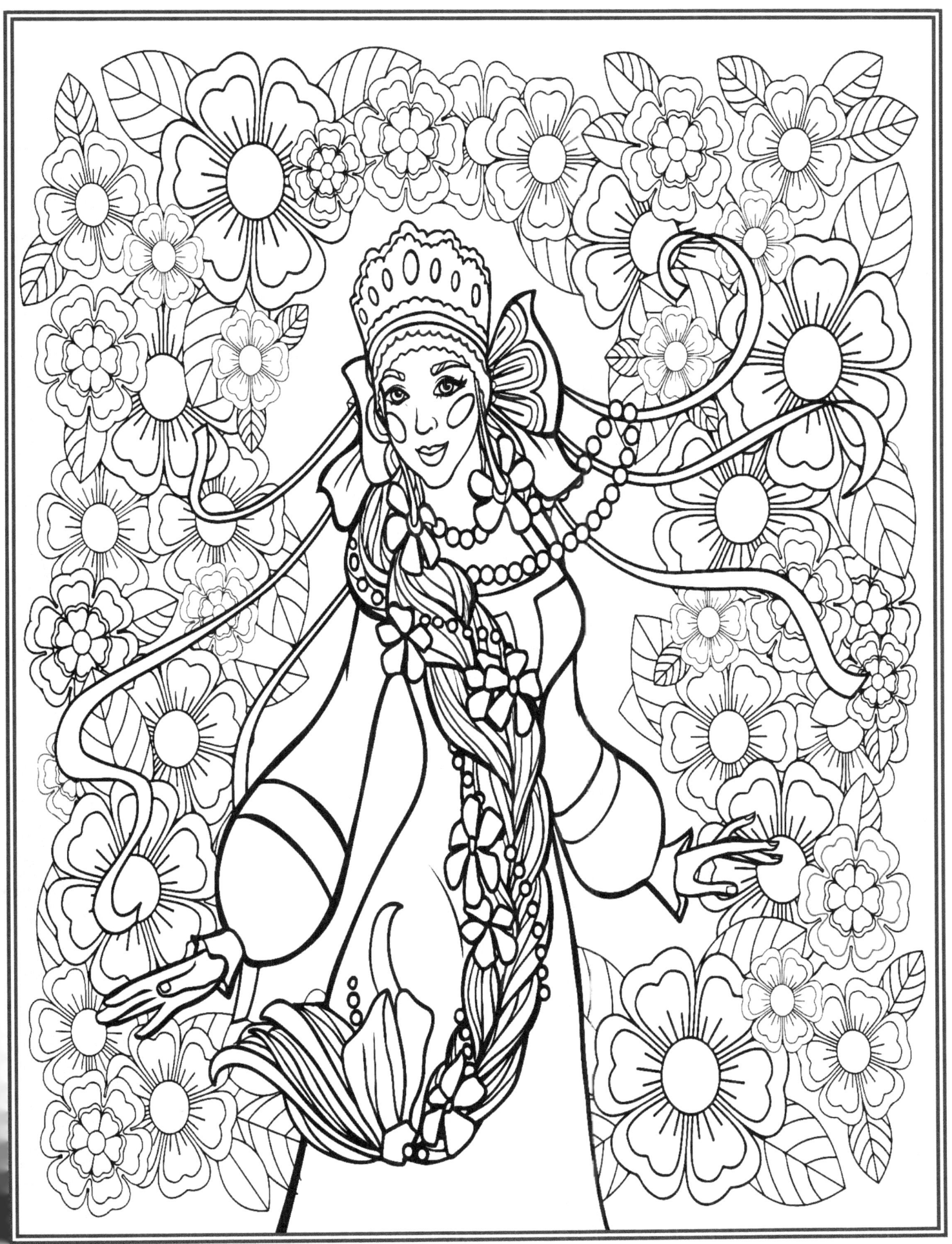

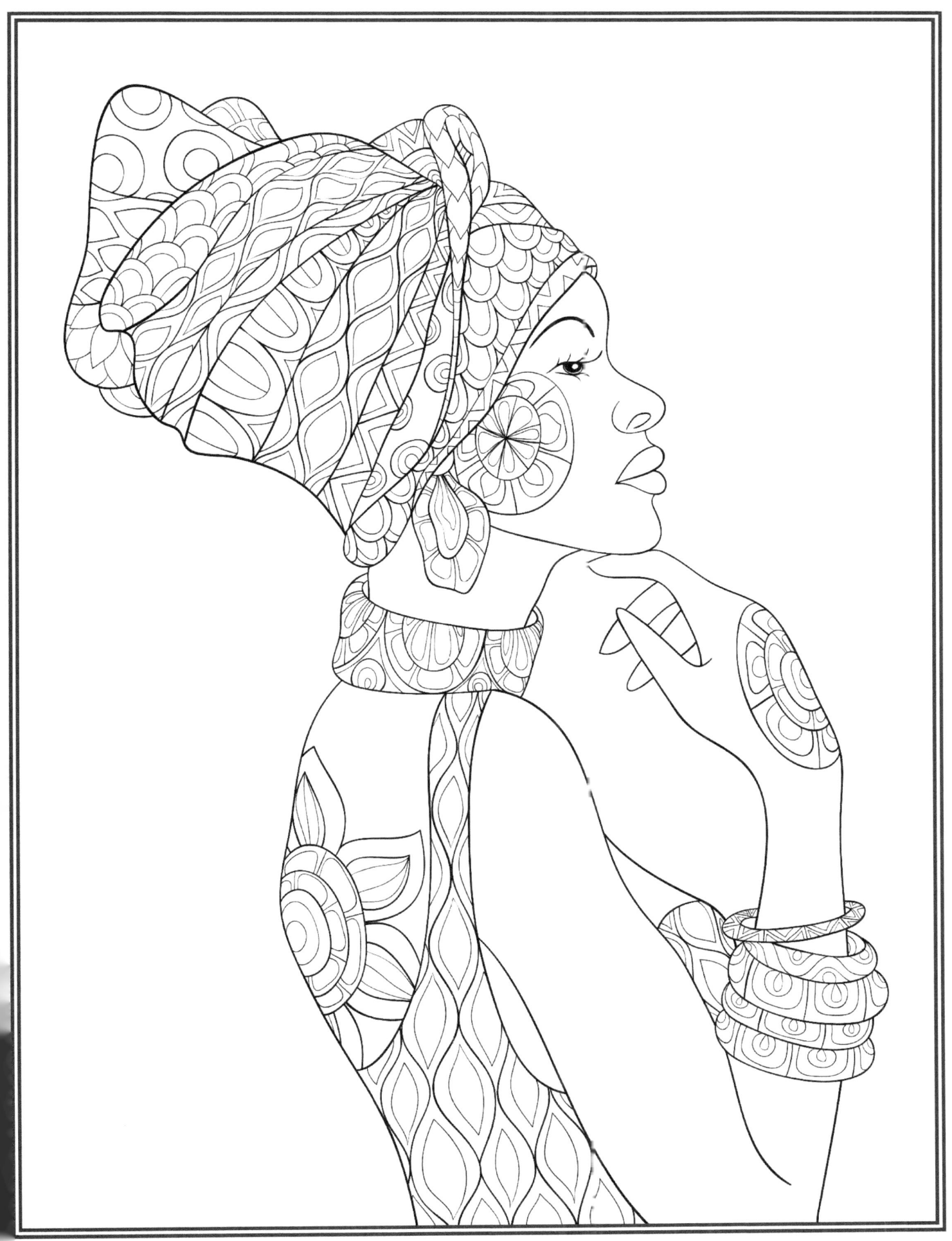

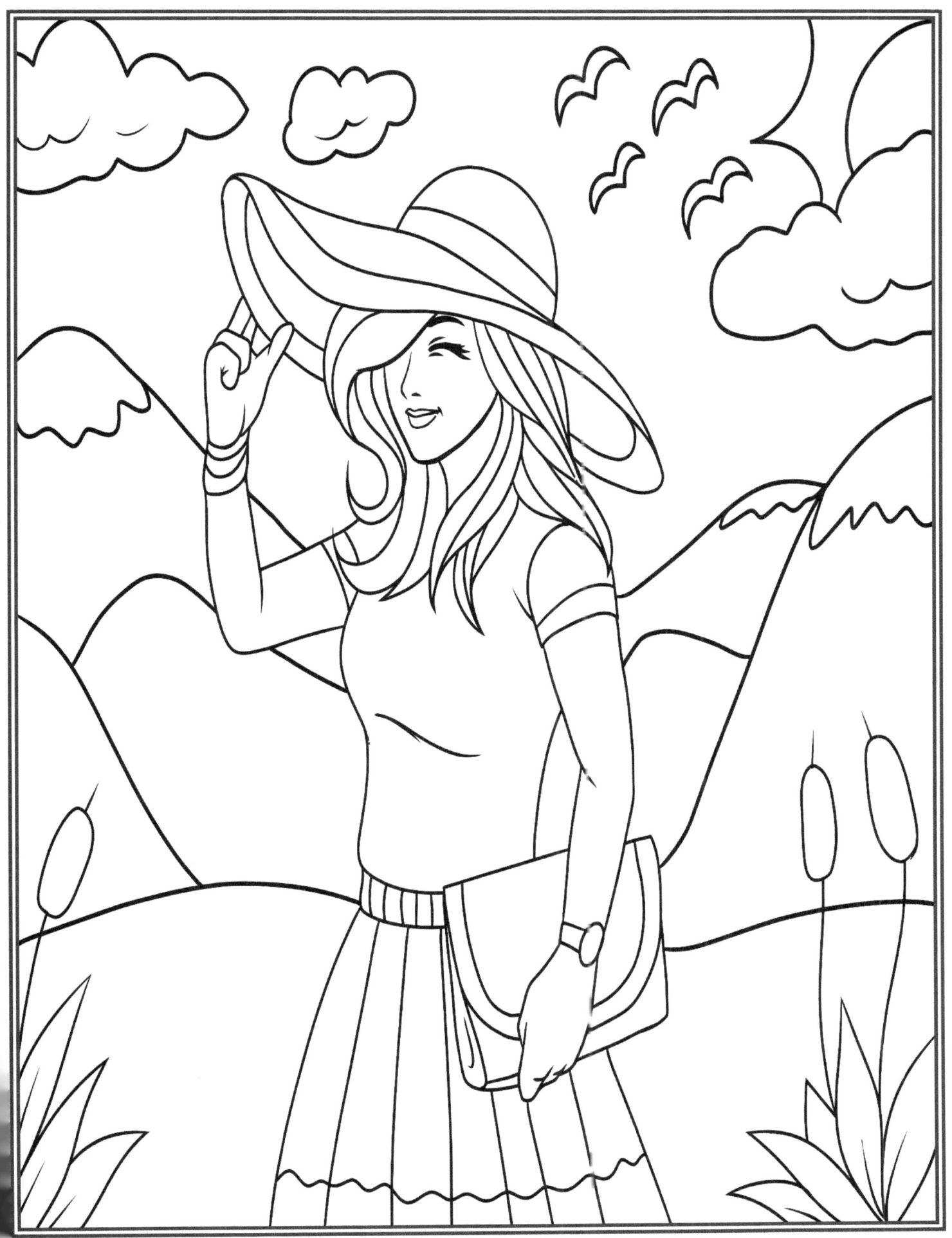

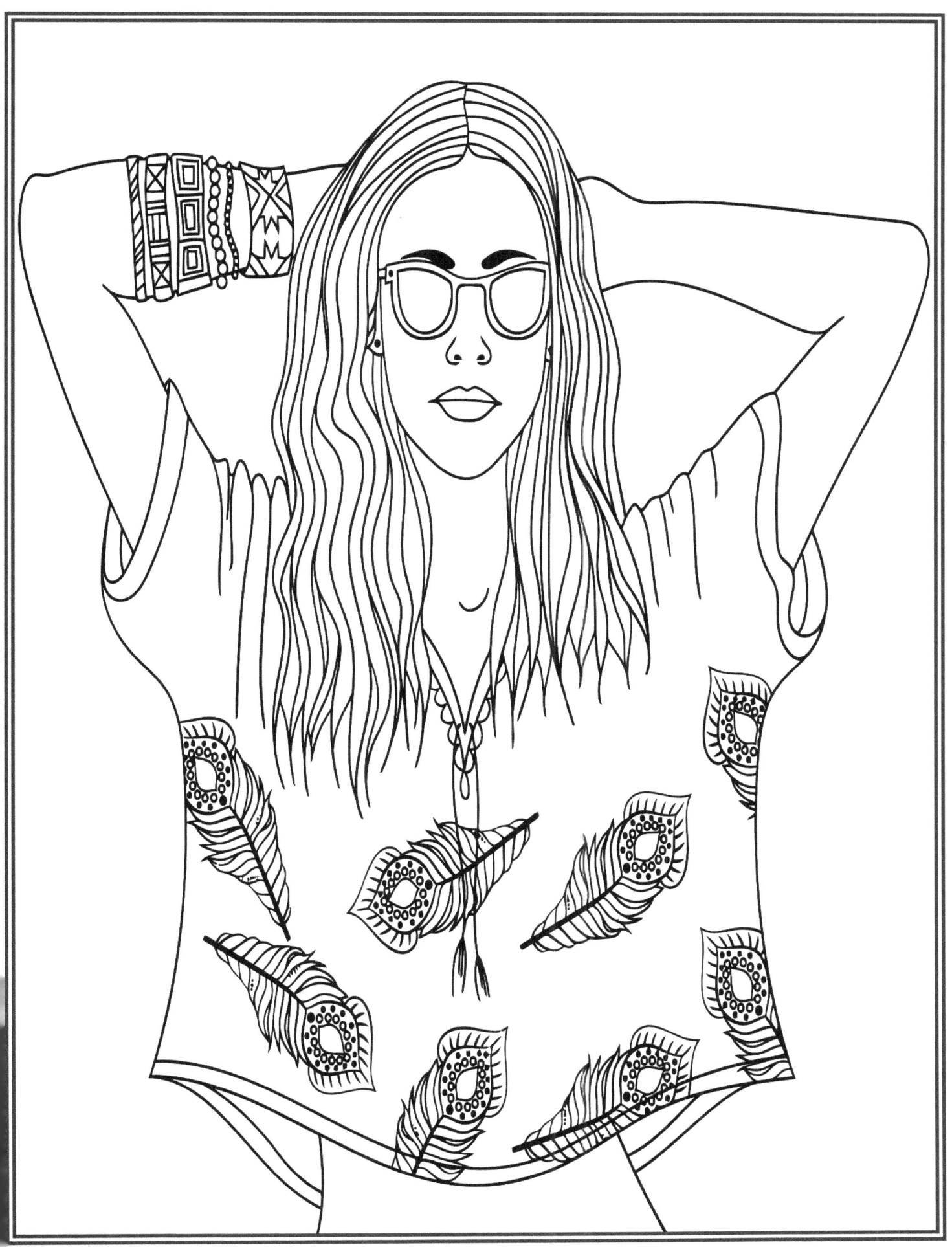

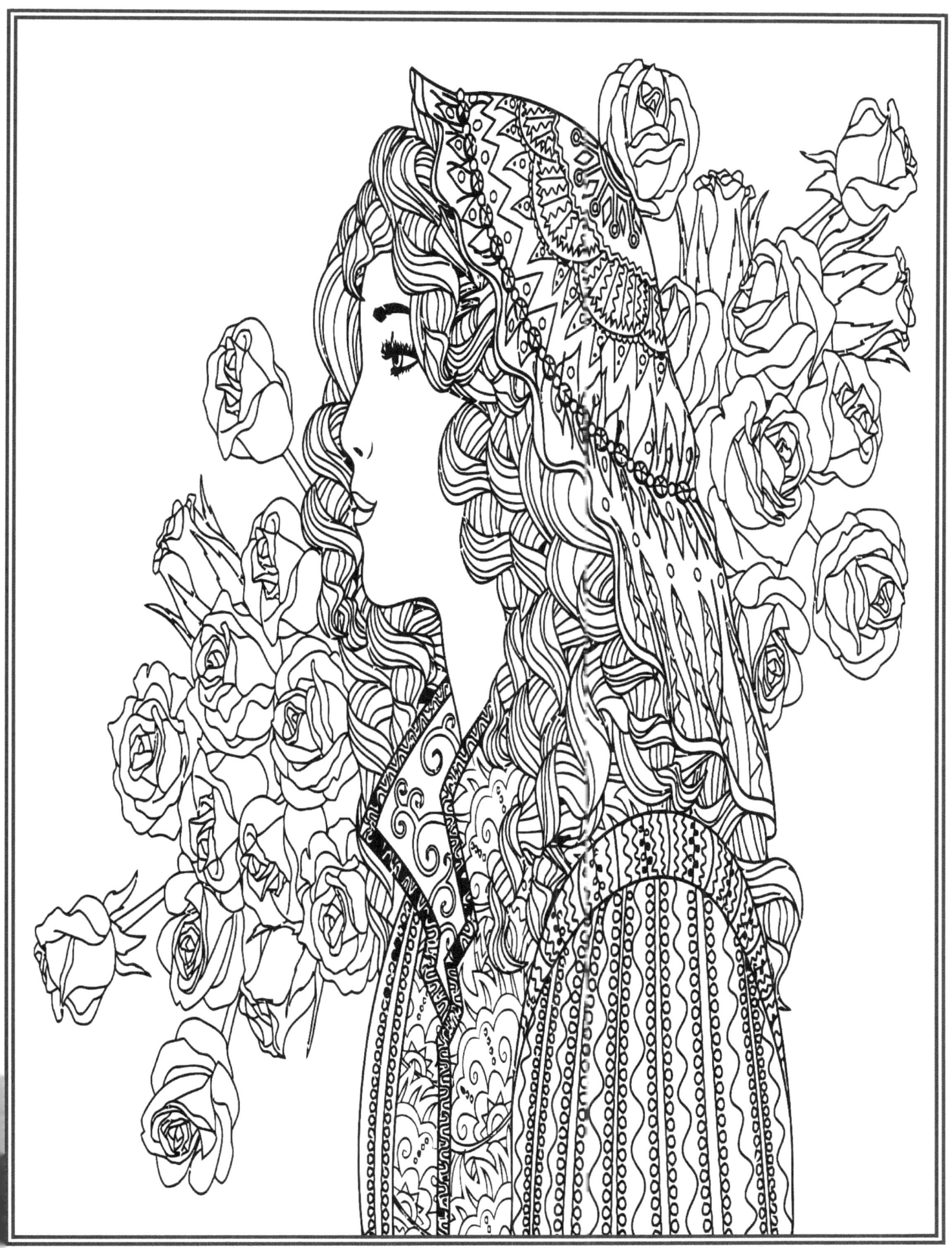

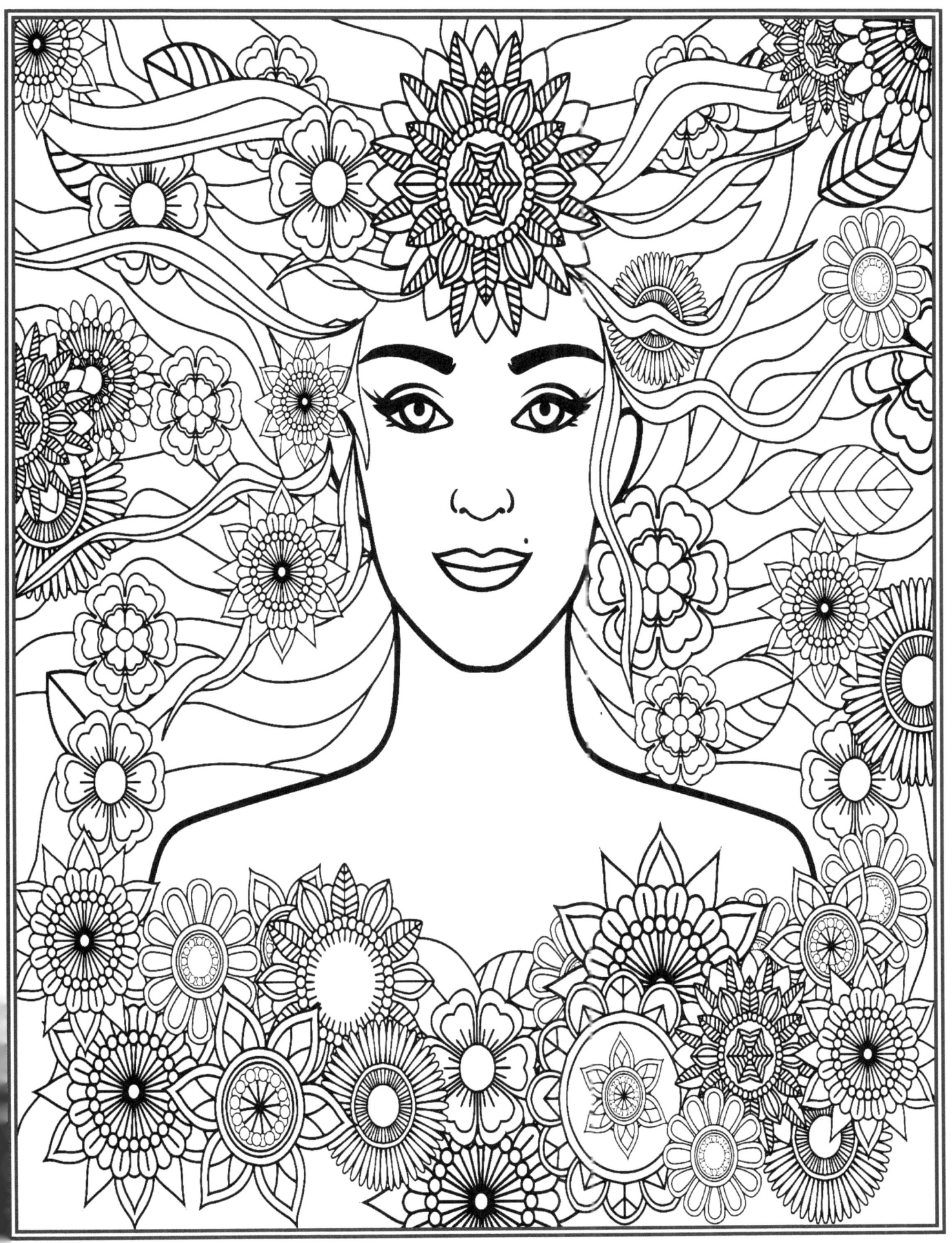

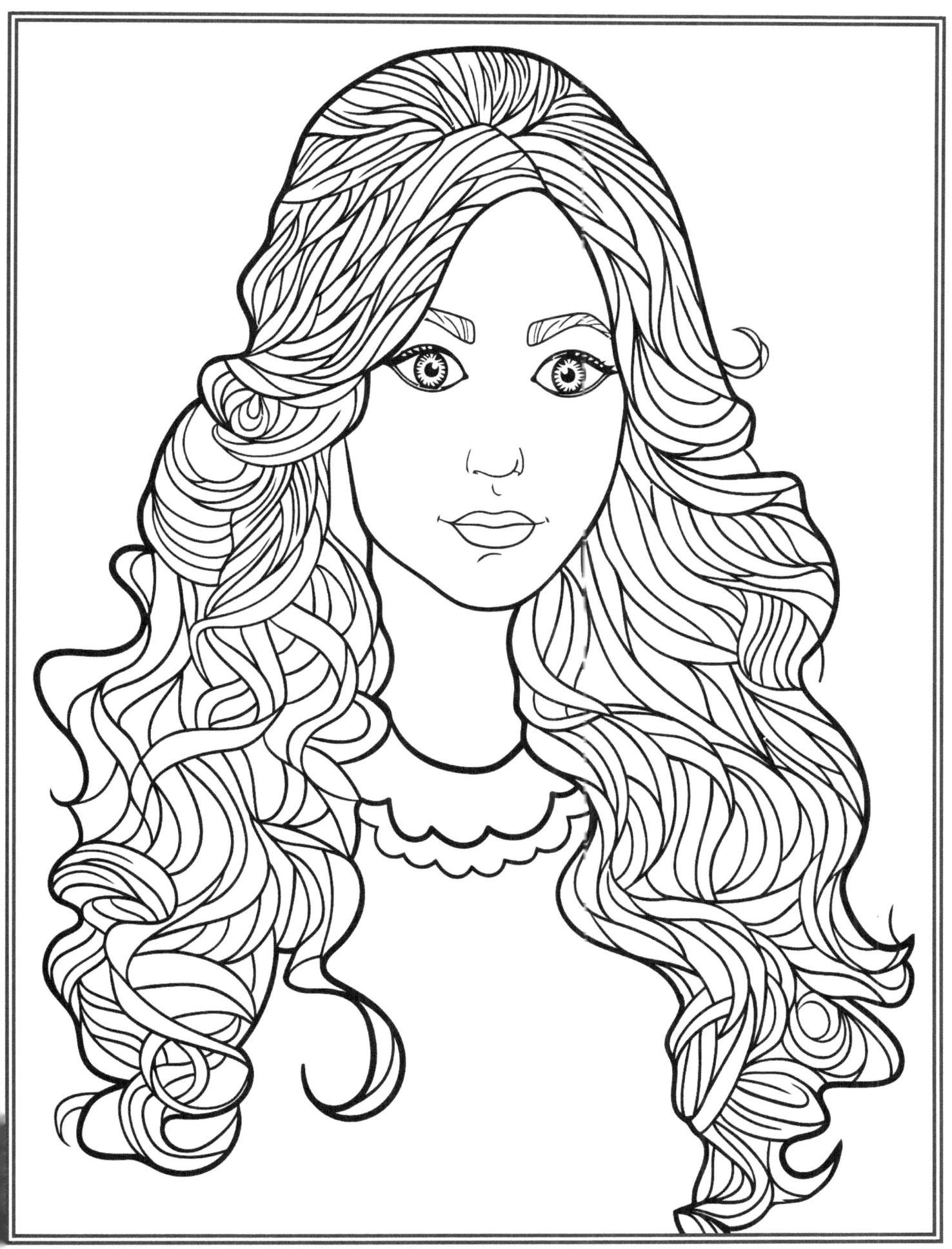

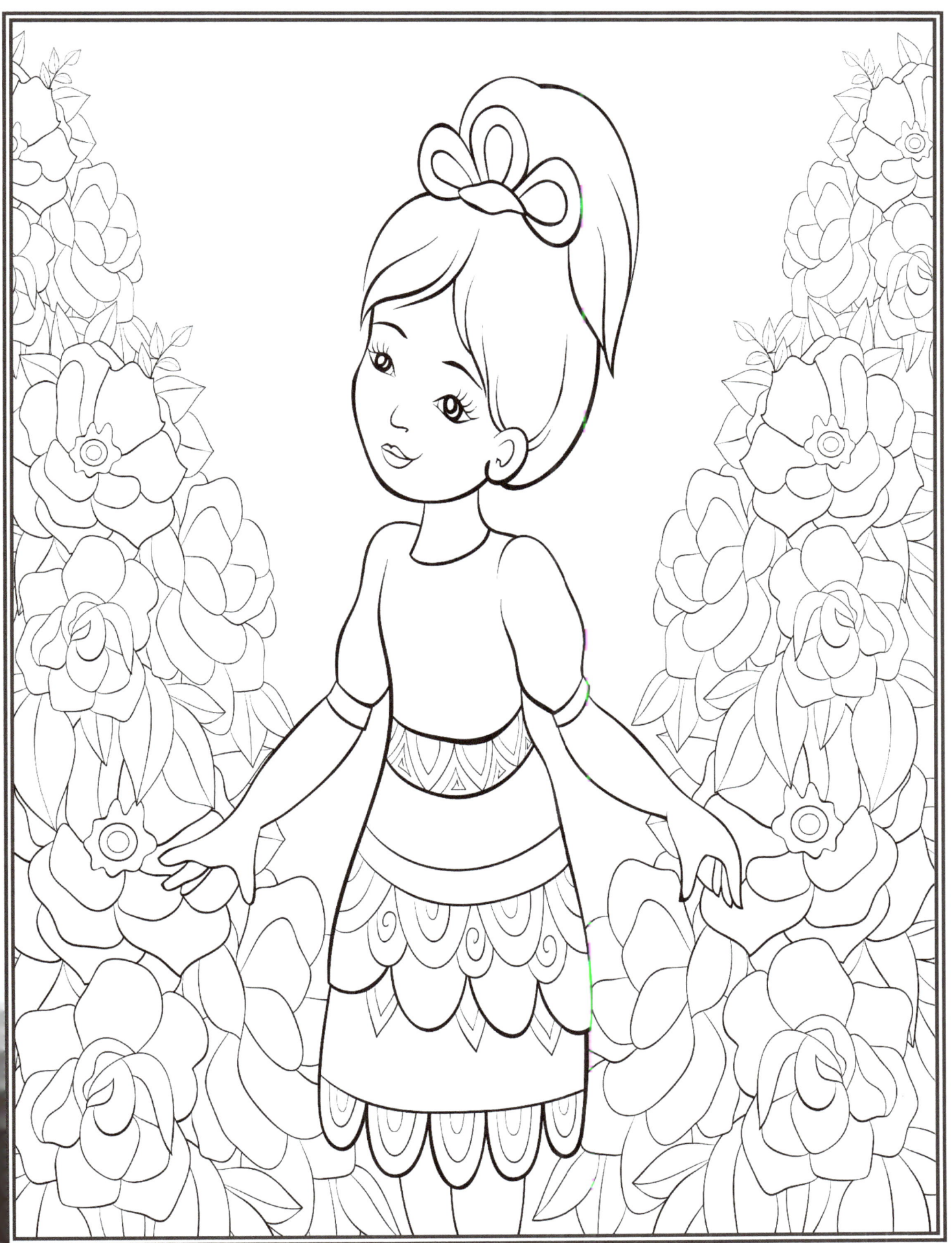

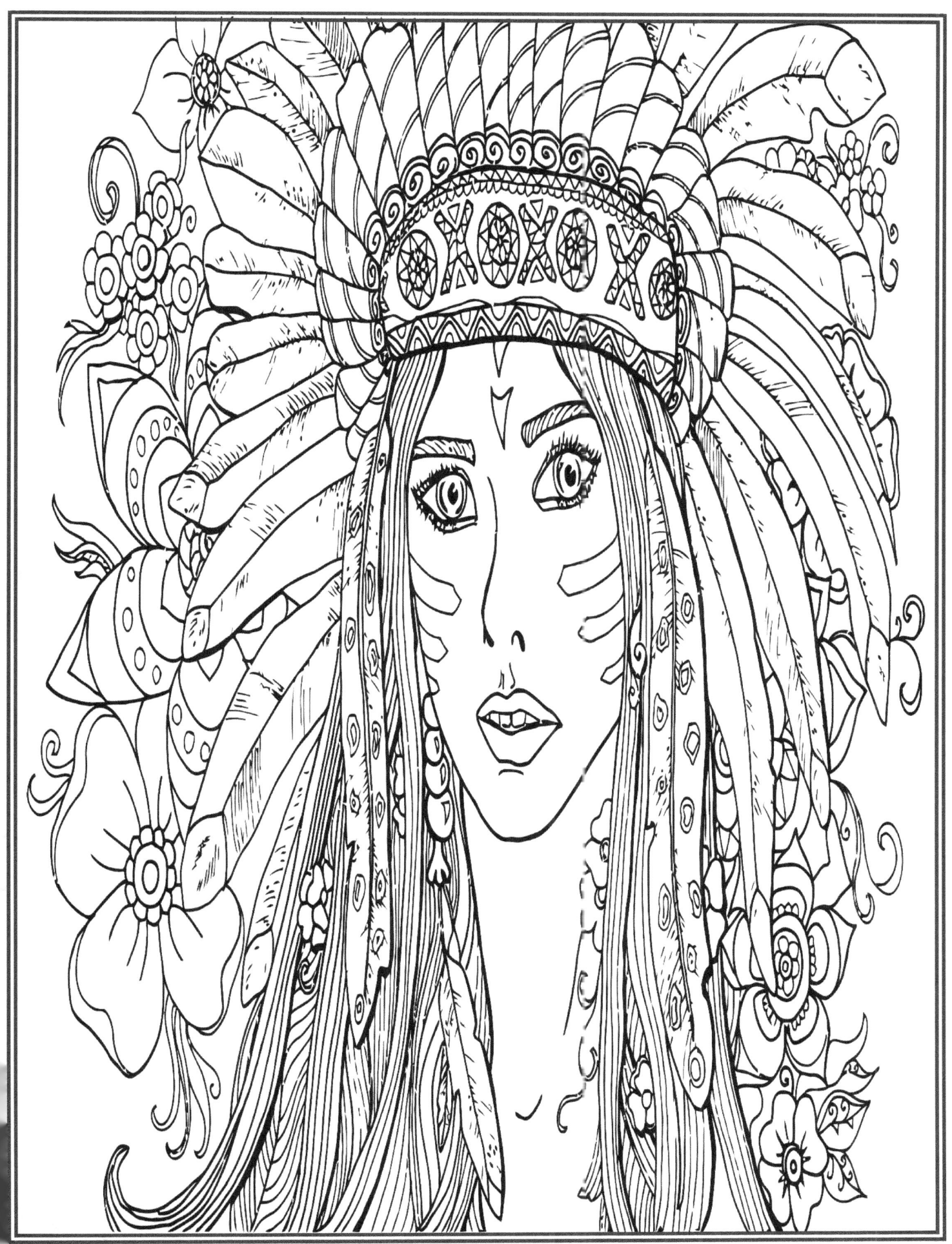

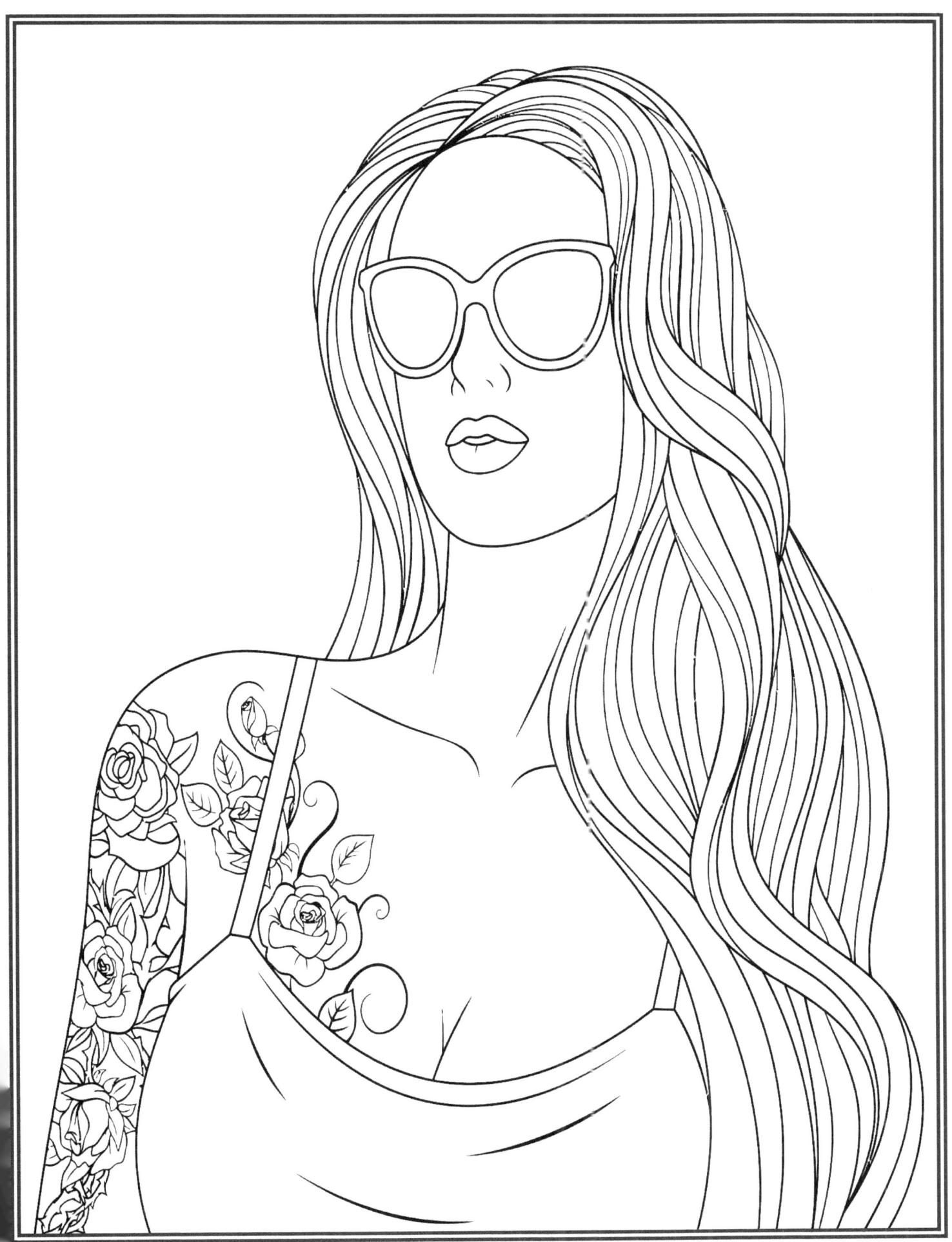

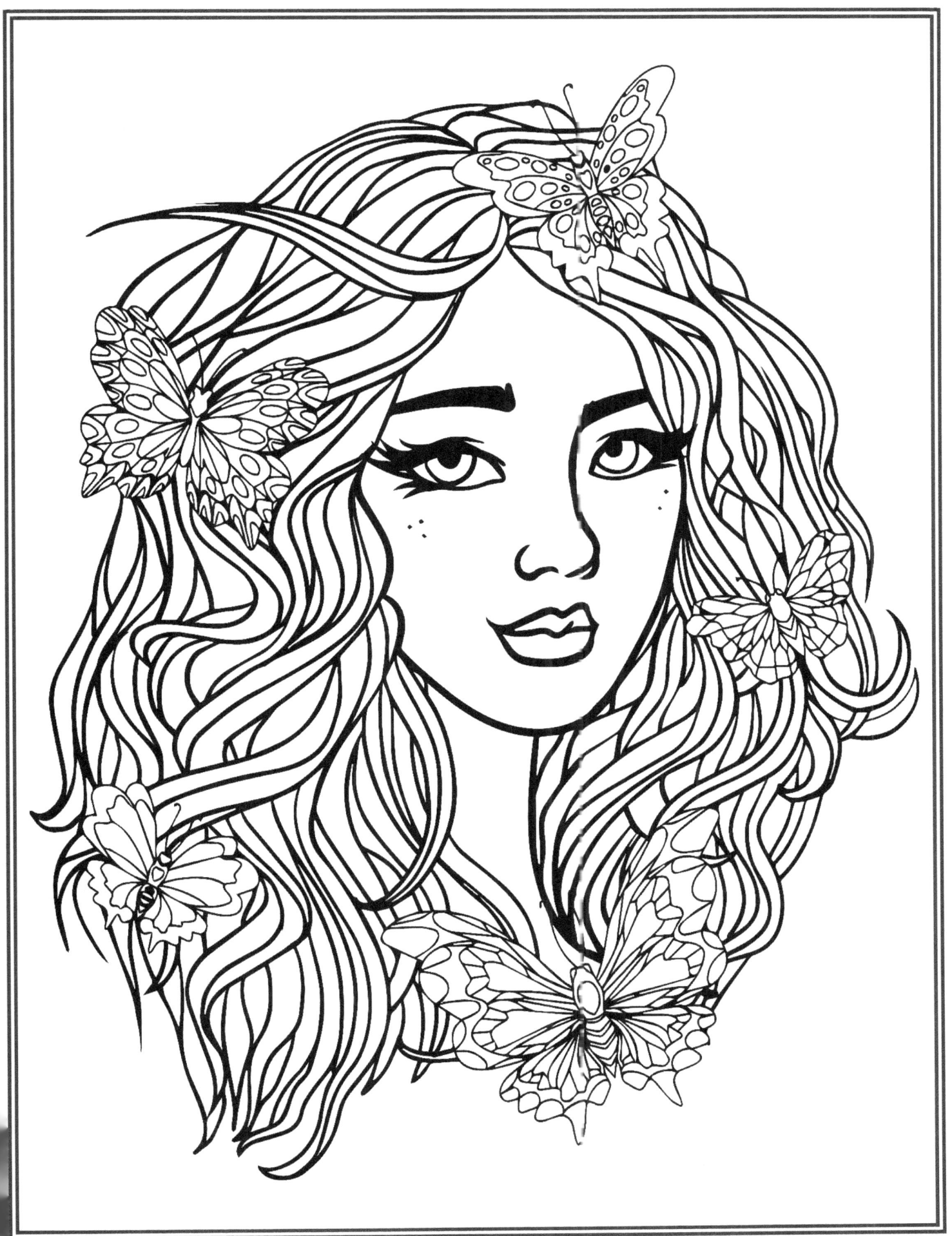

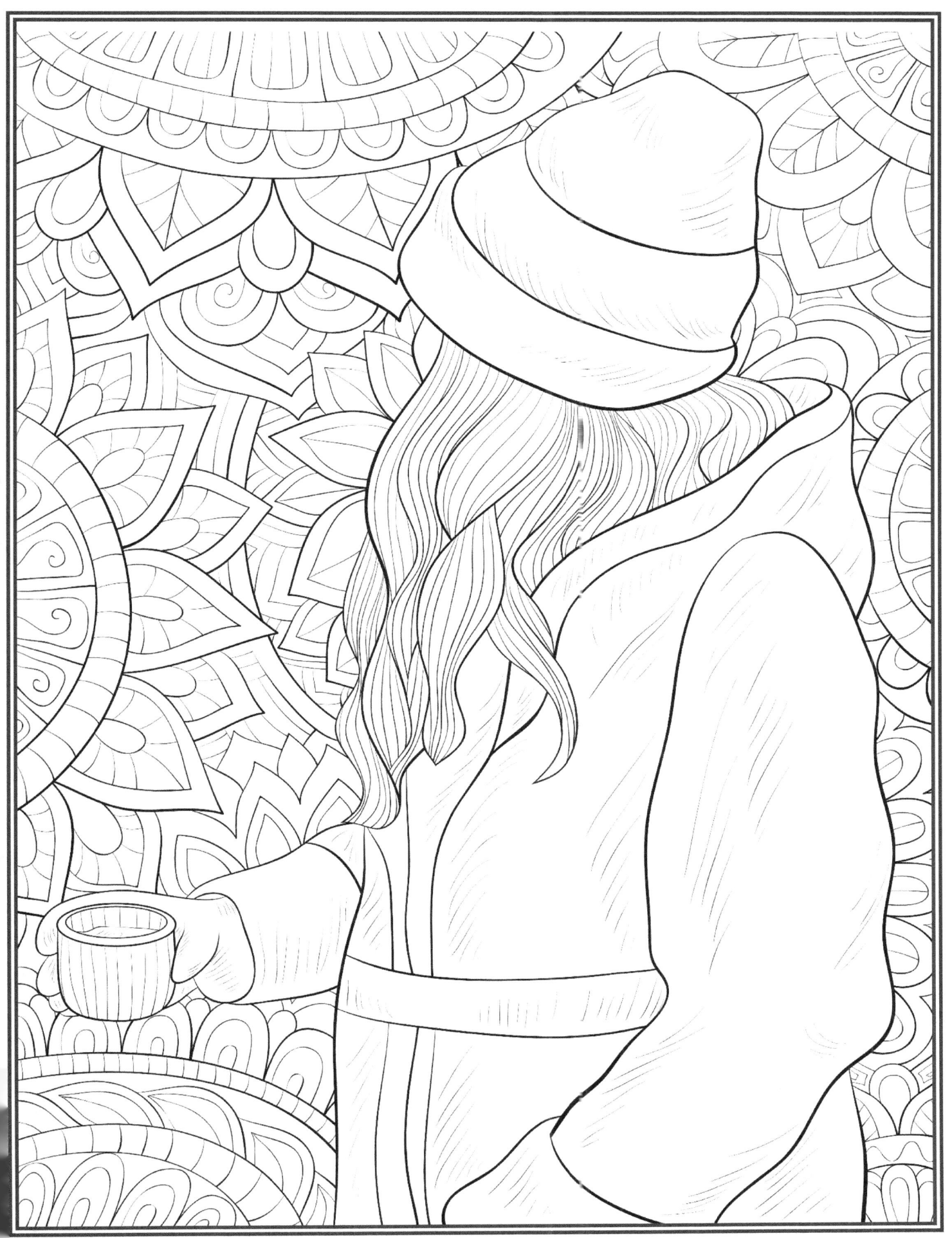

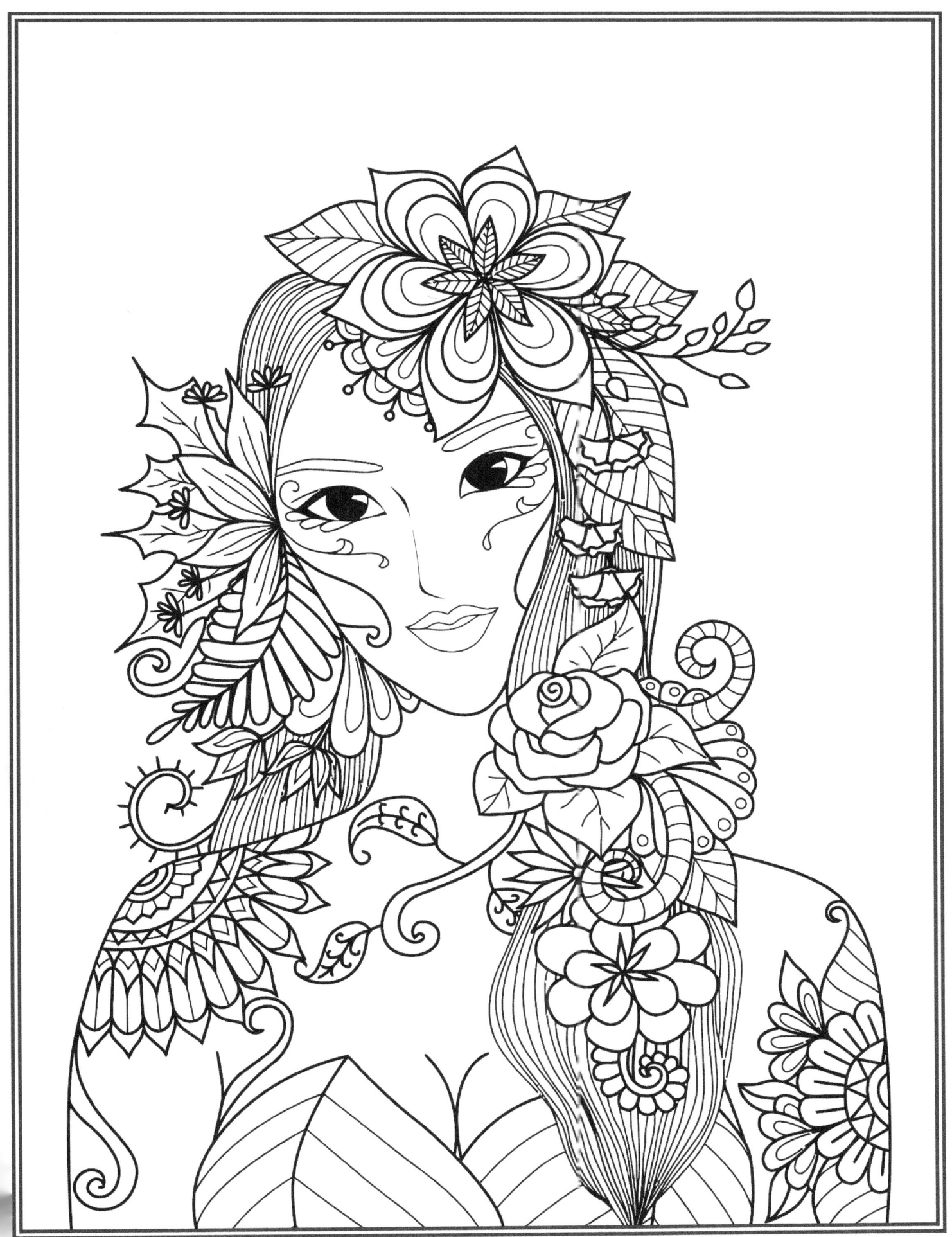

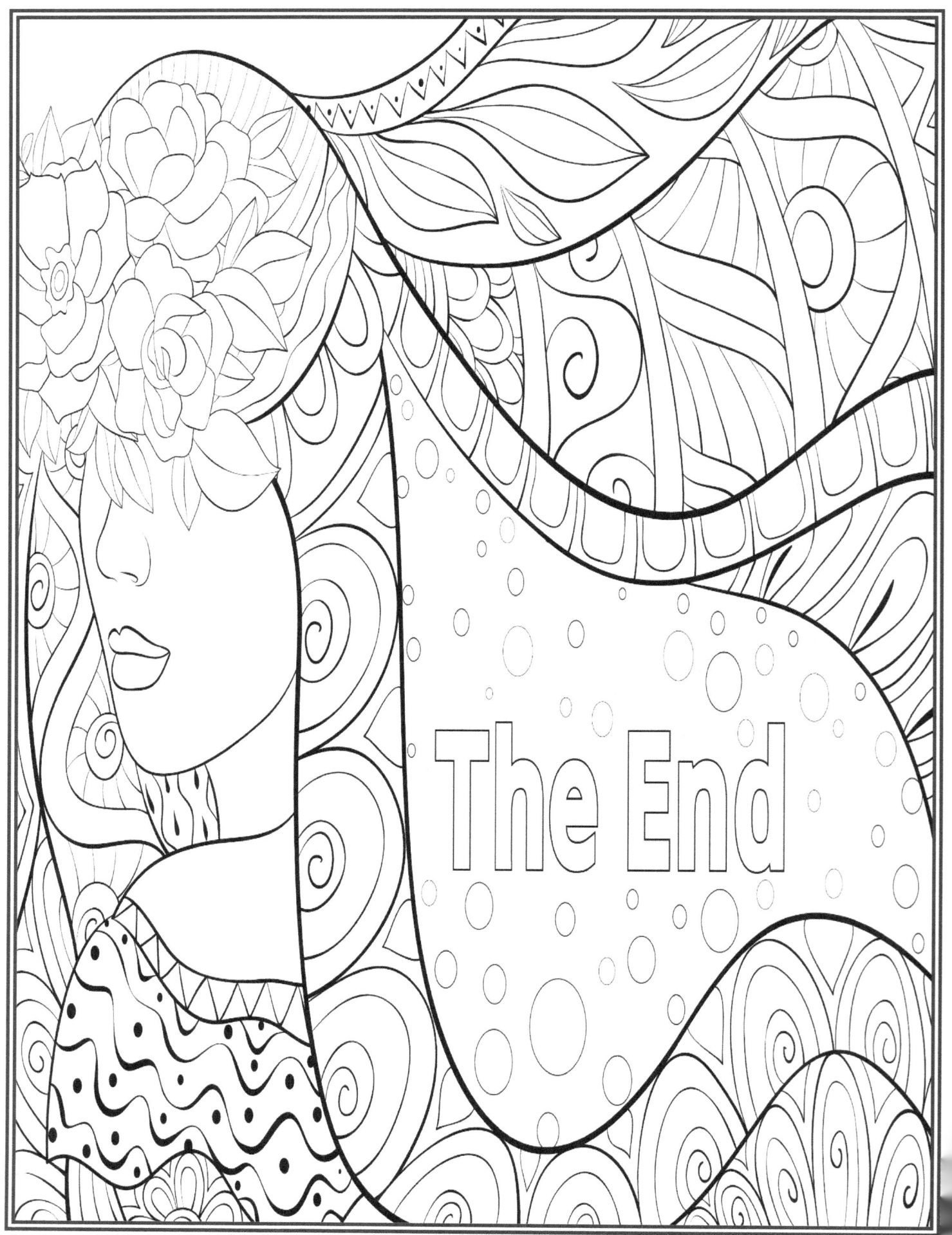

www.ingramcontent.com/pod-product-compliance
Lightning Source LLC
Chambersburg PA
CBHW080935220526
45465CB00008BA/3054